Samuel Parrish

Some chapters in the history of the Friendly Association for

Regaining and Preserving Peace with the Indians

Samuel Parrish

Some chapters in the history of the Friendly Association for Regaining and Preserving Peace with the Indians

ISBN/EAN: 9783337224912

Printed in Europe, USA, Canada, Australia, Japan

Cover: Foto ©Suzi / pixelio.de

More available books at **www.hansebooks.com**

SOME CHAPTERS

IN THE HISTORY OF THE

FRIENDLY ASSOCIATION

FOR

REGAINING AND PRESERVING PEACE WITH THE
INDIANS BY PACIFIC MEASURES.

———•••———

BY SAMUEL PARRISH.

———•••———

PUBLISHED BY

FRIENDS' HISTORICAL ASSOCIATION

OF PHILADELPHIA.

1877.

PREFACE.

SEVERAL years since, a "minute-book" of the "Friendly Association," and some papers pertaining thereto, were presented to me by a Friend—now deceased. From them, in large measure, the within account has been compiled. I have, however, availed myself of contemporaneous manuscripts, letters, &c. to elucidate portions of the narrative, and my thanks are due to those friends who have kindly furnished material to that end, or who in any way have assisted in the prosecution of the work.

To GEORGE J. SCATTERGOOD of this city, I am indebted for the loan of several papers from his valuable collection, and for information as to dates, &c. not readily obtainable elsewhere.

That errors and omissions, will be detected by the critical reader, notwithstanding the care taken to avoid them, is regarded as certain, but that these will be looked upon charitably, is confidently hoped.

The cut opposite, is believed to correspond in size and design, with the medal, alluded to on page 60 of the pamphlet.

"Friends' Historical Association" issue this incomplete history, that it may incite others to furnish data, if such there be, from which to trace the workings of the "Friendly Association" through the entire period of its useful existence.

THE AUTHOR.

NOTE.—In the Appendix are several papers, which, although not alluded to in the narrative, bear upon the subject considered therein.

SOME CHAPTERS,

IN THE HISTORY OF THE

FRIENDLY ASSOCIATION, FOR REGAINING AND
PRESERVING PEACE WITH THE INDIANS
BY PACIFIC MEASURES.

————•————

FRAGMENTARY information has occasionally been
printed, bearing more or less directly upon the
workings of the above-mentioned useful organization, but no exhaustive history of its proceedings
has yet been published. This is doubtless owing to
the fact that when the Association disbanded, its
papers were scattered among the members, whose
descendants either hold them as heirlooms of value
not to be parted with, or have destroyed them as
worthless. Thus it has happened, that after a lapse
of more than a century, sufficient material has not
been collected by any one person, so far as known,
to warrant the preparation of a complete narrative
of the beneficent labor, accomplished by this fraternity
of philanthropists.

The writer possesses an original "Book of Minutes"
of the Association, covering several years of its business in detail, as also letters and manuscripts, explan-
atory of certain matters contained therein. Portions
of these minutes, were used by S. Hazard in compiling

his " Register of Pennsylvania "; but there is much he has omitted, as irrelevant to his subject. From these sources, it is proposed to glean items of interest, in the hope that others, having similar information, may be induced to impart it. To Friends of this generation, who are striving to demonstrate the efficiency of "pacific measures," as a protection, alike to frontier settlers and Indians, this account, of what their fathers did in pursuance of the same ends, will, it is believed, be encouraging and instructive. It is a sad reflection, however, that notwithstanding the watchful care and self-sacrificing efforts of Friends and their co-laborers, the ancient glory of the red man, has passed away forever. The weak remnant of a once mighty race, cannot much longer, stem the ever-swelling tide of hostile immigration. Before the advance of civilization, the Indian reluctantly recedes. Where once he roamed the lord of the forest, stand towns and cities, the enduring monuments of Anglo-Saxon enterprise. Instead of the shrill war-whoop of ancient times, is heard the ceaseless hum of industry, and luxurious homes are erected, where lowly wigwams once stood. The waters, upon whose peaceful bosom, floated his light canoe, are now disturbed by the rapid transit of floating palaces, and through his hunting-grounds, the lightning train swiftly carries its human freight, from ocean to ocean. Sad is it, that the nation refused to profit by the wisdom of William Penn, who, in founding his colony, successfully joined *practical* Christianity with civil rule, in a "holy experiment"; but not in vain has the hand of friendship been extended to the Indian; not in vain have "the children of Onas" sought to avert the stroke of war, or to still the cry of annihilation, which has been sounded by some high in authority; upon them as peace-makers, will rest the promised benediction, whatever may be the result to the Indian.

Previous to the formation of the "Friendly Association" in 1756, some Friends, (who may be classed as among its most active members), had remonstrated earnestly against the governmental policy, which was undermining the old friendship between the settlers and the natives. The unprincipled conduct of many of the Indian-traders, (a fruitful source of trouble still), the repeated violations of solemn compacts, the introduction of "fire-water" among the Indians in the face of earnest protests from their chiefs, these, and kindred acts, induced Friends to interfere in their behalf. The Proprietaries of Pennsylvania, and the people generally were at variance, which added to the troubles of the colony. From 1733 to 1751, (eighteen years), eighty-three hundred pounds, or almost four hundred and sixty-one pounds per annum, had been expended out of the provincial stock, to defray the expenses of treaties designed to promote a good understanding with the Indians, thus paving the way for obtaining more of their land. This outlay, while burdensome to the people, materially enhanced the value of the proprietary estate, for by statute, Thomas and John Penn *monopolized the right of purchasing land.* These degenerate sons of the great founder of our Commonwealth, although reaping the largest benefits from treaties, persistently declined to bear an equitable share of their cost. Popular indignation was the result.

The Provincial Assembly, petitioned the Proprietaries under date of Sixth Month 23d, 1751. They declared substantially, that the government was based upon the principle of justice to all men, which assured the love and veneration of its people ;—that the Indians kindly supplied the wants of many destitute settlers, and as immigration increased, voluntarily retired to make room for their new guests, because, to use their own language, "*there was room for all*"; that the good faith kept with the *nearest* tribes gave the more distant Indians a favorable opinion of their white brethren ; that this friendship involved a very great expense to the people, but as the burden increased yearly, they were constrained to ask assistance of the Proprietaries, and hoped that their reasonable request might be granted. The fact that pecuniary aid could not *legally be demanded*, made the obligation stronger to bestow it, but the Proprietaries, refused to accede to the petition. About this time, also, differences had arisen between France and England, regarding the boundary between the British colony of Nova Scotia, and the French possessions in Canada. In 1753, the French erected a series of forts on the Ohio river, in order to protect their separated provinces of Canada and Louisiana. This was resented as an aggression by Great Britain, and in 1754 an English force under Major Washington, was sent to put a check upon the French operations. During this year, (1754) a grand treaty was held with the Six Nations, at Albany, when a purchase of land was made, for the Proprietaries of Pennsylvania. Charles Thomson, (afterwards secretary to the first Continental Congress) states, that for nearly a week, artifices were used, to induce the Indians to execute the deed of sale for a vast territory, which embraced the hunting-grounds of the Delawares and the Nanticokes, and the homes of the Shawnees and Ohio Indians. It was represented by the Proprietary agent, to the assembled Indians, "that unless they signed something of a writing to him for these lands, it would be taken for granted, that they had either sold them to the French, or intended to sell them to the people of New England, who had previously been in treaty with them for the same territory. In order therefore to remove that suspicion, some of the Indians were after much persuasion prevailed upon to sign the release, contrary to the established custom and usage of the Six Nations, not so much with a view of conveying the land, as to give the Proprietaries assurance, that they would not sell them to any other; yet even this release could not be obtained, without some private presents to particular Indians of known influence and authority."

Soon after this treaty, Conrad Weiser, provincial interpreter, was sent to the Delaware and Shawnese tribes, on the Ohio, to inform them of the purchase made at Albany, and, if possible, to explain that transaction. These tribes, however, declared they would not agree to the bargain. Subsequently, when one of the surveyors was sent by the Governor to lay out the land, "he was taken prisoner in an Indian town, detained until the next day, and, after divers consultations held there, was conducted back by a guard toward the English settlements, and made to understand that if he came again upon the same business, he should not be suffered to depart in the same manner."

Having endeavored to trace the causes which alienated the Indians from the settlers, it remains to show the action of Friends in the premises. In 1755, Israel Pemberton writes :—

" The frequent melancholy accounts of the barbarous murthers committed by Indians in the western and northern portions of this Province, filled the minds of people in general, with indignation and resentment against them, and no opportunity presented of publicly manifesting the earnest concern we had, to use our utmost endeavors, in a manner consistent with our peaceable principles, to prevent the impending desolation. The calamity became general, and every one was deeply interested in the measures taken, for enquiring into the causes which induced our ancient steady friends, to become our enemies. Yet this being the proper business of those then concerned in the administration of the government, we waited the event of their proceedings, having just grounds to hope, that the knowledge some of them had of several matters, which might proba- bly have contributed to this rupture, together with the repeated applications of the Assembly of the Province, would have incited them to pursue every rational method to end differences. Gover- nor Morris, however, determining to issue a declaration of war against the Delawares and Shawanese, many of the people called Quakers, residing in Philadelphia, met together, and after several weighty conferences, being sorely grieved with the present melan- choly circumstances of the Province, agreed upon an address to the Governor.''

This address was presented to the Governor, Fourth Month 12th, 1756, and on the following day he re- sponded thereto. In it, Friends remind him of Wil- liam Penn's administration, when truth, equity, and mercy prevailed, and mourn over the contrast as then existing. They announce their allegiance to the Prince of Peace, and, "while not presuming to prescribe," beseech the Governor to reconsider the proposed dec- laration of war, and to institute a rigid inquiry, as to " whether some apprehensions these Indians have con- ceived, of a deviation from the integrity of conduct towards them, so conspicuous in the first establishment," may not have assisted, to alienate their affections. Friends also declare their readiness to do what they can, to secure peace, even *to the extent of contributing more money* " *than the heaviest taxes of a war can be expected to require*," as an evidence of their sincerity. They conclude this able appeal as follows :—"May the mind of the Governor, be endued with that wisdom, which the wisest of kings experienced to be better than weapons of war; and may thy councils be directed to the honor of God, and the good of the people over whom thou presidest, is our sincere desire and prayer."

The Governor replied, that he and his Council had reconsidered the declaration of war, and that after serious discussion, the Council advised him, immediately to issue his proclamation of war, which being in accordance with his views, he should do, so soon as he could make proper distinction between friends and enemies.

This answer led Friends to petition the Assembly, then in session, to which body they enclosed a duplicate of their address to the Governor. They urged the Assembly to remember "the emphatic and prophetic declaration of the wise, worthy, first Proprietor of this Province, viz., 'if Friends here keep to God, and in the justice, mercy, equity, and fear of the Lord, their enemies will be their footstool; if not, their heirs and mine too will lose all, and desolation will follow.'" They appeal to the Assembly by their "sacred and civil obligations, to add their endeavors, to effect the necessary and salutary measures of peace."

Friends then had an interview with Conrad Weiser, as one conversant with Indian affairs, and had their apprehensions confirmed, that the natives felt aggrieved, because their lands had been taken from them without adequate compensation, and because some settlers presumed to occupy territory, for which no negotiation had taken place. Weiser asserted, that the only method "to save the Province from ruin, was to endeavor for a peace with them, by pacific measures," and highly commended the efforts of Friends in this direction. A few days subsequently, Weiser sent

William Locquies, (a friendly Delaware Indian then in the city), to Israel Pemberton, with a note recommending him as a suitable messenger of peace, to his disaffected brethren. A number of chiefs of the Six Nations, were also in Philadelphia at this time, and Friends thought it necessary to show them some mark of favor. Anthony Benezet and Israel Pemberton, waited upon the Governor, to apprise him of their design towards these chiefs, which he acquiesced in, after the assurance from them, that if anything of public interest should transpire, he should be promptly acquainted therewith. These Indian chiefs, with Conrad Weiser, Andrew Montour (interpreters), and D'Claus (Sir William Johnson's secretary), dined at Israel Pemberton's with a few Friends. After dinner, a free conversation occurred on public affairs, and the Indians asked for another meeting, whereupon Governor Morris was informed by Israel Pemberton, of the peaceable disposition of these chiefs. Speaking for those assembled at the meeting, Israel said, they desired that at a future interview, the Governor would advise and direct the manner of proceeding, and that as the provincial treasury was well nigh depleted, Friends were prepared to supply him with five thousand pounds, if needed, with which suggestion the Governor was much pleased. Israel Pemberton further remarks:—

"About twenty of us, with the same interpreters, had two more conferences with the Indians, and the most material parts of what they said were afterwards communicated to the Governor, and the proposal made by Scarroyady, of sending three messengers—Newcastle, Jiggera, and William Locquies—to the Delawares and Shawanese settled about Wyoming, being approved by him, the necessary provision was made for their setting out, and proper company provided for their safe conduct through the improved part of the province.

When they were ready to proceed on their journey, the Governor being waited on, by Israel Pemberton and William Logan for the passes, and being requested to direct what signal they should give on their return, to distinguish them from enemies, while the passes lay before him ready to be signed, he suddenly appeared to change his intentions, and signified his resolution to consult his Council on the occasion. The minutes of our conversation with these Indians being examined, and signed by the three interpreters, were immediately after this delivered to the Governor, and his Council being summoned, we were informed, they soon agreed that as he had so lately declared war, any offers of peace from him would be unreasonable, and that the method first proposed, of the messengers going with such instructions as they had received from their own chiefs, was most fit to be pursued. The next day, Scarroyady, Jonathan, and the other chiefs, setting out in the stage-boat for New York, after they were gone, the messengers refused to perform the service they had undertaken, and the day following the Governor, in consequence of some intelligence received from the Governor of New York during these conferences, concluded to send the messengers in his own name."

He furnished them with a message to their people, urging them to lay down the hatchet, and expressed his willingness to meet them, at some place mutually agreed upon, in friendly conference. These peace-makers started on their journey to Wyoming, by way of Bethlehem, in the latter part of the Fourth Month, 1756. They returned on the 31st of Fifth Month following, and made report that on their arrival at Wyoming, it was discovered the Indians had gone to Teagon (Tioga). Thither they repaired, and informed their friends, that the Governor of Pennsylvania had sent them a message, which was read in council a few days after their arrival. Paxinosa, a chief, made answer as follows :—

" BRETHREN, THE GOVERNOR AND PEOPLE OF PENNSYLVANIA :— The dark clouds overspread our country so suddenly, that we have been all at once separated, for that dark cloud got in between us; but it has pleased the Most High to dispel it a little, so that we can just see one another again. Our eyes are now running with tears, because of the melancholy sight, seeing our country covered with your and our blood. Give me leave to wipe off the tears from your eyes, though at the same time, my own run with tears in abundance, for what has passed.

"Brethren, as you came a great way and through dangerous places, where evil spirits reign, who might have put several things in your way to obstruct your business, this string (of wampum), will serve to clear your mind, and the passage from your heart to your mouth, that you may speak freely to us."

Teedyuscung, a Delaware chief, spoke next, as follows:—

"BROTHER ONAS AND THE PEOPLE OF PENNSYLVANIA:—We rejoice to hear from you, and that you are willing to renew the old, good understanding, and that you call to mind the first treaties of friendship made by Onas, our great friend, deceased, with our forefathers, when himself and his people first came over here. We take hold of these treaties with both our hands, and desire you will do the same, that a true friendship may be re-established. Let us both, take hold of these treaties with all our strength, we beseech you. We, on our side, will certainly do it. Brother Onas, what you said to us we took to heart, and we speak to you from our heart, and we will deal honestly with you in every respect. Brother Onas, we desire you will look upon us with eyes of mercy. We are a very poor people. Our wives and children are almost naked. We are void of understanding, and destitute of the necessaries of life. Pity us."

"THE DELAWARES, MINISKIES (MINISINKS), AND MOHICKONS TO ONAS AND THE PEOPLE OF PENNSYLVANIA:—Brethren, there is a great number of our people among you, and in a manner confined. We desire you will set them at liberty, or rather give them a safe conduct to Wyoming, where we intend to settle, as at your fireside. There, we will with you, jointly kindle a council fire, which shall always burn, and we will be one people. Brother Onas and all the people of Pennsylvania, we had the misfortune, that a great and dark cloud overspread our country. But by our prudence, and that of our uncles, the Six Nations, it is now almost dispelled, and we see the clear heavens again. We, the Delawares, the Shawanese, the Mohickons, and Miniskies (Minisinks), give you this string of wampum, and desire you that the bitterness which might have gathered in this dark and unhappy time, may be removed, and that you may by this means, spit it out. Take or accept this, as a certain cure for that purpose. Think on your poor foolish brethren with mercy, and forget all the evil done to you by them. Brother Onas, what our uncles, the Six Nations, required of us in your and their behalf, by their delegates at Otsaningo, we who live on the River Susquehanna, have agreed to. We have laid aside the hatchet, and will never make use of it any more against you or your brethren, the English. All our young men have been consulted about this, and all earnestly agree to it, and we now speak in their presence. We must caution you, not to charge them, with anything that may be done by the Ohio Indians, who are under the influence of the French, against you. We assure you, our young men will do no more mischief to your people."

During the absence of the messengers aforesaid, Israel Pemberton sent letters to Sir William Johnson, and Sir Charles Hardy Governor of New York, in order to secure their co-operation, and that of the Six Nations, in the restoration of peace. Israel Pemberton states, that "Governor Hardy kindly sent an answer, evidencing his hearty concern for the public welfare, and laying us under sensible obligations, and we have never received the least hint from General Johnson, of his disapprobation of our conduct. Under these circumstances, we have reason to apprehend that our intention was approved."

Governor Morris was so well pleased with the result of the conference held at Tioga, that on the 8th of Sixth Month (1756), he sent Captain Newcastle, Jiggera, and several more Delaware Indians, with a second message to their brethren, the most important item in which, is as follows :—

"As you have laid down the hatchet, and desire the same may be done by us, our messenger carries with him, our proclamation for the suspension of hostilities within the limits therein specified, of which we have informed the Six Nations."

Israel Pemberton, in commenting upon the events then transpiring, says :—

"From the time of the first messengers arriving at Teaogan, the *hostilities on our northern frontiers ceased*, and an acceptable respite being obtained for our distressed fellow-subjects, we enjoyed so much real pleasure and satisfaction, *in the happy event of our endeavors*, as to engage us, cheerfully to pursue the business we had begun, though many malicious calumnies and aspersions were cast upon us, by persons from whom we had a right to expect encouragement and assistance."

On the 19th of Seventh Month (1756), Captain Newcastle and his companions, returned to Philadelphia from Tioga, with the information that Teedyuscung, the Delaware King, and some thirty of his people, were in waiting at Bethlehem to see the Governor, or if he desired, they would come to Philadelphia to confer with him. He at once notified the Assembly of this fact, which body, appointed two commissioners to accompany the Governor to the treaty, and appropriated three hundred pounds, to defray their expenses. Captain Newcastle also stated to several Friends, that the Indians having heard that " the children of Onas " *were the first to propose and promote pacific measures*, it was important, for a few of them to attend the coming treaty, taking with them some things necessary for the relief of the Indians, as a peace offering.

"On the 20th of Seventh Month, several Friends met, and unanimously agreed, that it would be necessary to enter into a subscription to raise a sum of money, to defray the charges which have already arisen, and what will now immediately become necessary, and likewise to provide such a fund, that on future occasions we may be able to promote the interest, welfare, and peace of our country, by contributing toward the expenses of treaties with the Indians, in such manner as may appear to be most conducive of the public good, and tend to improve the confidence the Indians have repeatedly, and especially of late, expressed in men of our peaceable principles. And after several conferences, on the 22d, the following preamble of a subscription was agreed to, viz.:—'We, the subscribers, from a consideration of the necessity of regaining and promoting the friendship of the Indians, who were the native inhabitants of this country, and being in hopes the pacific measures lately proposed may have that good effect, in order to demonstrate our hearty concern, to maintain the principles of peace and good-will we have professed to them, and to contribute our assistance towards so important a service, in a manner consistent with our peaceable principles, do hereby promise and oblige ourselves, our heirs, executors, and administrators, to pay unto Anthony Morris, John Reynell, Jonathan Mifflin, Jeremiah Elfreth, Jeremiah Warder, Israel Pemberton, Joseph Morris, William Fisher, Charles Jones, James Pemberton, Joseph Richardson, Abel James, Thomas Say, Joshua Emlen, Owen Jones, and Samuel Sansom, or their order, the sums by us respectively subscribed, within twelve months after date hereof, together with lawful interest for the same, to be employed for the purposes aforesaid ; and we do agree, and direct the said persons before named, within four months after date hereof, to appoint a time and place for a general meeting of all the subscribers, and notify the same by an advertisement in the "Gazette," or otherwise, in order that at such general meeting a Treasurer and Trustees be appointed for executing this trust, and for regulating their trust, authority, and duty, and a proper method be settled in which the Treasurer and Trustees may be obliged to render their accounts annually, and be made answerable for such sums of money as may be contributed for the purposes aforesaid.' Upwards of twelve hundred pounds were immediately subscribed. It was like-wise agreed that some goods be purchased by Jeremiah Warder, Abel James, and Israel Pemberton, and a wagon hired to convey them to the place where the treaty is to be held, and that as many

Friends as can go, be encouraged to attend it. After which Israel Pemberton waited on the Governor, and acquainted him of our intentions of waiting upon him at the treaty, and taking with us a small present for the Indians. On the 23d, the goods being provided, were sent by Henry Shettle's wagon, and upwards of twenty Friends set out on the journey, and on the 24th arrived at Bethlehem, where we were informed that the Indian King and his company were waiting at Easton, in pursuance of the Governor's first directions, and that the Governor, his Secretary, and one of his Council were gone thither to meet them.''

" On the 25th we went forward to Easton, and soon after our getting there, Anthony Morris, John Evans, William Brown, and Israel Pemberton waited on the Governor, and acquainted him that twenty Friends and upwards were come from Philadelphia, in order to contribute what may be in our power towards promoting the work of peace, which we are desirous of doing, in a manner agreeable to the Governor.

"At the Governor's lodgings we first saw Teedyuscung, who, on our coming in, immediately expressed his regard for and confidence in the *Quakers*. We afterwards called and shook hands with him at his lodgings, and he expressed great satisfaction in seeing us, and said Newcastle had told him of the Quakers, and that they would come to meet him, which he now found to be true, and that now he saw them he felt it to the point of his heart, and should not say anything to the Governor unless the Quakers were present. To avoid giving offense we did not stay five minutes with him. Soon after our coming to town, we were informed that the Governor had given orders that no person should speak with the Indians, and a guard was set near their lodgings to prevent it. The Governor and his attendants, about ten o'clock, attended their public worship, where Parson Peters, his Secretary, preached to them. In the afternoon, Friends had a satisfactory meeting in the same place, at which Benjamin Trotter, John Evans, and William Brown had very seasonable and acceptable service, and there appeared some grounds to hope the minds of many would be suitably prepared for the succeeding business. In the evening the wagon with our goods arrived, which were deposited in a vacant house where we had liberty to lodge, the blankets intended for the Indians serving us for beds.

" In the evening the Indian King and most of his attendants came uninvited and supped at our inn, from whence with some difficulty we persuaded them to return to their lodgings immediately after supper, without taking a drop of strong liquor, and they promised wholly to refrain from it, that the next day they might be fit for business.

"26th of Seventh Month. This morning Newcastle and Pumpshear, acquainted us that the Indian King and his company, who had been drinking intemperately several days before, were now sober, and the King said his head and heart were clear and ready to enter on business; and they freely expressed their sentiments on several matters which they expected would be the subjects of public consideration, with which they desired the Governor might be informed. In pursuance of which the substance of what was said was communicated to W. Logan, of the Governor's Council; but Conrad Weiser not being yet come, the Governor determined to defer treating with the Indians till he came. Newcastle and the interpreter Pumpshear being sent for by the Governor, and desired to give their sentiments on several matters, answered freely as to most of them; but as to some particulars begged leave to refer the Governor to what they had already said to Israel Pemberton, with which they presumed the Governor was, or would be acquainted by one of his Council, with which the Governor seemed highly displeased, and charged Pumpshear to inform said Pemberton, and by that means all the Quakers in town, that he should treat them as his Majesty's enemies, if they held any conference with the Indians on any matter relative to the government, and that he had strictly charged the same to be observed by all persons whatsoever, on his first coming."*

"The interpeter then informed him that we had been particularly cautious in that respect, and, so far as he knew, clear from any conversation with them; and after giving the reasons for the conversation, he and Newcastle had voluntarily entered into with said Pemberton, one of which was the difficulty of free access to him at suitable times, the Governor's wrath seemed to abate, but he enjoined them in future immediately to communicate to him or to his Secretary, or to some of his Council, and to no other, anything

---

* Israel Pemberton says:—"At this time, and at all times before and since the treaty, the Moravians at Bethlehem are allowed to entertain such Indians as they please, and to have the liberty of freely conversing with them, though the Quakers in this arbitrary manner are forbid, at the time the Governor knew they came solely to promote and assist in the restoring peace; and the lower class of people are permitted to curse, swear, and rail at them, and endeavor to incense them against us within their hearing, which appears to be very offensive to them."

they might have to say, and promised them free admittance at all times. The Governor's message and conduct, appeared so extravagant, that Pumpshear did not, before the next meeting, deliver the message. The Indians this day dined with the Governor, and his Council and attendants, and we were informed that the King after dinner, in a full and pathetic manner, expressed his concern for the mischief which had been done. This raised tenderness towards the Indians, in most who were present.

"After this, we thought of inviting the Indians to dine with us, but on hinting it to one of the Governor's Council after he had spoken with the Governor, we were informed that it was not approved, and we therefore declined it. Captain Reynolds from Fort Allen, this day informed us he had intelligence there were about twenty Indians seen in that neighborhood, by which some of the people were much alarmed, and had fled from their plantations, upon which we renewed our application that messengers might be sent to invite those Indians to come in, being a party left behind by Teedyuscung, who we were apprehensive, might, by his staying longer than expected, be tempted to commit some irregularities, but we could not succeed therein.

"27th of Seventh Month. Conrad Weiser arrived, but the Governor went out fishing, and the Indians spent the day in drinking so much, as to render them unfit for business. In the morning Friends met together, and agreed to attend to the service we were engaged in, and that no one should depart without first notifying his intentions to the company, and obtaining consent. Near forty of us are now together. It was likewise agreed, that Anthony Morris, John Evans, William Brown, and Israel Pemberton should wait upon the Governor and acquaint him, that by a message received from him yesterday by John Pumpshear, we perceive he is apprehensive that we have had, or intend to have, some conferences with the Indians now come to town, relative to the affairs of Government ; and therefore we think it necessary to inform the Governor, that we have not had any such conferences with them, and to repeat what we said when we first waited on him, that our sole purpose in coming and waiting here is to be assistant, so far as may be in our power, in promoting the work of restoring peace, in a manner consistent with our stations and circumstances, and the respect due to him as our Governor. In the evening, the said four Friends delivered the message, with some of the reasons of our coming up, &c. The Governor positively denied that he had sent us any message by

Pumpshear, treated us civilly, and repeatedly assured us of receiving with pleasure, and duly considering any hints or intimations we might think proper to give, of such matters as might appear to us necessary to be regarded on the present occasion; but of our intended present to the Indians he did not take the least notice. We hinted the apprehensions we had of the Indians suspecting our being deficient in regard to them, as to avoid offense we had declined seeing or speaking with them, excepting the interviews at our first coming, and the short time they unexpectedly spent in supping with us; and we found that Captain Newcastle and the interpreter, were both much concerned to find us laid under such restraint."

"28th Seventh Month. We had notice this morning of the Governor's intention of speaking with the Indians, and by attending at the time and place and crowding ourselves in, obtained admission and kept minutes of what was said by, and to them. In the afternoon, some of us visited the Moravian settlements at Nazareth, Christians Brunn, and Gnadenthal, and were highly delighted with the œconomy of the families, and with the extraordinary improvements of every kind, which, notwithstanding their infancy, much exceed anything in America."

"29th Seventh Month. The Governor again met the Indians, and we obtained admittance as at first, and kept minutes of most that was said, though the hasty and inconsiderate method in which the Indians' answers were received, rendered it impracticable to be as exact as the importance of the occasion and subject required. In the evening Friends met together and agreed that Anthony Morris, John Evans, William Brown, and Jonathan Mifflin should again wait upon the Governor, and repeat the assurance we had before given, of our desire to promote the business in which he is engaged, in the manner most agreeable to him, and to let him know we desire his consent to our delivering a present to the Indians, or that he would be so kind as to deliver it for us, as a testimony of our regard for them and of our hearty desire to improve the confidence they have said they have in us, to the public benefit. On their return they informed us that the Governor declared positively, that he would not permit Friends to deliver their present to the Indians, nor did it appear to him proper that he should do so; but that he would consult his Council and give us a positive answer in the morning."

" 30th of Seventh Month. The Governor, by one of his Council, notified us that if we would consent to put our goods, with those provided at the public expense, he would deliver them with the following speech, viz.:—

" ' BRETHREN :—I acquainted you yesterday, that the people of Pennsylvania had put into my hands a small present, to relieve you, your wives and children, in their present distresses. I now think it necessary further to inform you that a part of this present, was given by the people called Quakers, the descendants of those who first came over to this country with your old friend William Penn, as a particular testimony of their regard and affection for the Indians, and their earnest wish to promote the good work of peace in which we are engaged.' On consideration, it is unanimously agreed that we should consent to the Governor delivering our presents ; but in order that the Indians may know what part of the goods were provided by Friends, that a list of them be delivered to the interpreter, to be communicated to them when he has a suitable opportunity. And a string of wampum was provided to be delivered by the Governor, with the speech he has promised to make on delivering the goods.

" 31st of Seventh Month. An express having arrived from Philadelphia, last evening, with news of Lord Loudon's arrival at New York, and the declaration of war against France, the Governor determined this day to declare war, and afterwards to close his conferences with the Indians, &c. Accordingly, at 12 o'clock, after the declaration of war, the Governor delivered the presents, closed the conferences, and invited all the Indians, and others, to dine with him. About one hundred and fifty of us dined under a booth, the Governor behaving with great civility and openness, in a manner which gave universal satisfaction. Most of the people called Quakers, intending this afternoon to set out homewards, immediately after dinner took leave of the Governor and Teedyuscung, at which time the King, addressing himself to us all, said, viz., ' Now we have made this good beginning of the work of peace, I desire you may let it be known to all your people, far and near. I will do the same among our people. I hope you will hear of no more mischief being done. If I should hear of any being intended against you, I will do my utmost to give you notice of it, but do not let this cause you to be off your guard. Perhaps some of the Ohio Indians may come over the river without my knowing it, but if I do know, you shall certainly be informed of it.' "

During the treaty, several Friends who could not conveniently attend it, were employed in soliciting subscriptions in the city, and elsewhere, and about one thousand pounds had been contributed. But owing to an unfounded rumor, that the Indians, after their departure from Fort Allen, "made a cantico, and burnt all the goods presented to them," Friends deemed it advisable, temporarily, to suspend collections. In the Tenth Month, 1756, information was received that Teedyuscung, with about one hundred Indians, and four or five prisoners, were in the vicinity of Easton, and it was thought important by Friends, to give aid in promoting peace, and securing the release of the prisoners. William Denny was now Governor of Pennsylvania, but because of some misrepresentations made to him by Secretary Peters and some of his Council, he declined to confer with Friends concerning the Indians, and insisted on their reducing to writing, all propositions which they desired to make. It was therefore concluded by a few city subscribers to the above-mentioned fund, to call a *General Meeting* of Friends, "on Third day afternoon, at 3 o'clock, the 2d of Eleventh Month, at the great Meeting-House, in this city. Israel Pemberton, undertakes to notify Aaron Ashbridge, of Goshen, Thomas Carleton, of Kennett, and George Miller, of Providence, in Chester county. Joseph Morris, to notify Abram Dawes and John Morris, of Plymouth, in order that they may inform contributors in their respective neighborhoods." Lists were made of all the city contributors, which were divided among a committee, and the form of a notice was agreed on, to be delivered to each contributor, or to be left at dwellings. It was agreed by the few Friends assembled at this informal meeting, to propose to the general convocation, that a Treasurer, and twelve Trustees be chosen by ballot.

On the second day of the Eleventh Month, 1756, the Association, it may be said, was organized. The Indian question had been brought to the attention of the Yearly Meeting, by a few zealous Friends, but that body considered any interference with "*public affairs*" as beyond its jurisdiction, and declined action. This decision, although unexpected to the Friends who had undertaken to aid the Government, in all measures calculated to promote peace with the natives, was not disheartening, and the meeting on the 2d of Eleventh Month, was an endorsement of their labors. There were present on that occasion, the following contributors to the fund, as taken from the minute-book :—

From Chester county—Aaron Ashbridge, Isaac Howell, Thomas Lightfoot, Jr., and George Miller. From Berks county—Benjamin Lightfoot, Francis Parvin, and John Starr. From Philadelphia county—Abram Dawes, John Eastburn, and Andrew Zeigler. From the city of Philadelphia—Nathaniel Allen, Anthony Benezet, William Brown, Davis Bassett, James Bringhurst, Joseph Baker, Samuel Bissell, John Bissell, John Care, John Cresson, John Cowpland, Jonathan Carmalt, William Cooper, William Clark, Thomas Crosby, William Craig, Joseph Davis, John Drinker, John Drinker, Jr., Henry Drinker, Joshua Emlen, Jeremiah Elfreth, Joshua Fisher, William Fisher, Samuel Grisley, John Gillingham, Isaac Greenleafe, Joshua Howell, Benjamin Hooten, Caleb Hewes, Abel James, James James, Charles Jones, Owen Jones, Edward Jones, Aquilla Jones, Jacob Lewis, Thomas Lightfoot, William Lightfoot, Jonathan Mifflin, Joseph Morris, Samuel Preston Moore, Abram Mason, George Mifflin, Joseph Mariot, Samuel Noble, Robert Parrish, Thomas Paschall, Israel Pemberton, James Pemberton, John Pemberton, Peter Reeve, Samuel Rhoads, John Reynell, Joseph Richardson, Francis Rawle, Hugh Roberts, Samuel Sansom, Henry Shute, Thomas Say, William Savery, Joseph Saul, Jacob Shoemaker, Jr., James Satterthwaite, Christopher Thompson, Jeremiah Warder, Robert Waln, Daniel Williams, Richard Wistar,

Samuel Wetherill, Thomas Williams, Peter Worrall, Isaac Zane—eighty-three Friends in all.

At this meeting, Israel Pemberton gave a narrative of what was done at the conferences with the Indians at Easton, of the presents purchased at the expense, and given in the name of the contributors, of the rumors which hindered further application for contributions, of a second conference at Easton, and of " the opportunity now offering of more extensive service than heretofore," and recommended the—

" Choosing of a Treasurer and Trustees, to receive such sums of money as have been, or may be subscribed towards promoting the good work proposed, and bringing it to the desired issue, after consideration of which, and the conduct and proceedings of the Committee being approved, it was agreed at this meeting to choose a Treasurer, and that the former Committee be continued till the next general meeting, and that it is necessary that as many of them as can attend the approaching conferences at Easton, with as many others of the contributors as can be engaged to go, should be there.

" Agreed that the committee should purchase as many goods for clothing the Indians, as they, on consideration, may think proper, if, on applying to the Governor, they find he is willing to present them to the Indians in our name, in the same manner the former Governor did.

" Samuel Preston Moore, Samuel Rhoades, Hugh Roberts, Jacob Lewis, Richard Wistar, Thomas Crosby, Abram Dawes, and Daniel Williams are desired, in conjunction with the committee, to make an essay of rules, necessary for the orderly management of our business, and for regulating the trust, authority, and duty of the Trustees and Treasurer, to be brought to our next General Meeting, at which time it is agreed that sixteen Trustees should be chosen by ballot.

" John Reynell, was now chosen Treasurer by ballot, after which, the General Meeting, adjourned till the first day of next month, at 10 o'clock, at Friends' schoolhouse, in this city."

On the 3d of Eleventh Month, 1756, the committee met at the house of Israel Pemberton, and prepared an

address to the Governor, which was presented to him
by six Friends, who reported they were favorably received, and that the Governor would answer the communication promptly. The following are copies of the
address and answer :—

" *To William Denny, Esq., Lieutenant-Governor and Commander-
in-Chief of the Province of Pennsylvania, &c.:*

"The address of a considerable number of the people called
Quakers, in the city of Philadelphia, for themselves and their
brethren in other parts of the said Province, showeth, that the
calamities and desolation of our fellow-subjects on the frontiers of
the Province, having been the painful subject of our frequent consideration, with desires to be instrumental towards their relief by
every means in our power, consistent with the peaceable principles
we profess, some of us, had by the permission of Governor Morris,
some conferences last spring, with some Indian chiefs of the Six
Nations, from whence we are confirmed in our apprehensions, that
there was a prospect of some good effect, by further endeavors to
promote pacific measures with the Delaware Indians, on the northern
frontiers of this Province.

"That immediately after the conference, Governor Morris sent a
message to these Indians, in which he particularly mentioned our
earnest desires to interpose with the Government, to receive their
submission, and establish a firm and lasting peace with them.

"That from the accounts given us by the Indians who delivered
this message, we were informed that the Delawares, reposed great
confidence in the continuance of our endeavors to that purpose,
and after the receipt of a second message, some of them, were induced to meet Governor Morris at Easton, and there, laid the
foundation of a more general treaty. That a considerable number
of us, attended the said treaty at Easton, and from the conduct and
express declarations of the Indians, were assured that our personal
attendance, was very acceptable to them, and conducive to the
general service.

"That in confirmation of the sincerity of our desires to promote
the restoration of peace, we had provided a present of such clothing
for these Indians, as they appeared to be immediately in want of,
which Governor Morris was pleased to deliver them, in our behalf.

" That as we are now informed, a much larger number of Indians
are waiting to meet the Governor at Easton. Being still desirous
of promoting the restoration and establishment of peace with them,
we are ready and willing by personally attending the treaty, to
manifest the continuance of our care and concern herein, and our
hearty disposition to regain and improve the friendship of the
Indians, to the general interest of our country ; and if our furnish-
ing a supply of clothing for them, against the approaching winter,
in addition to what is provided at the public expense, may in any
measure tend to these purposes, and be consistent with the Governor's pleasure, we shall cheerfully provide and send them to the
place appointed for the treaty, to be delivered them by the Governor,
in such manner as will most effectually promote the public service,
and express our friendly disposition towards them. All of which
is, with much respect, submitted to the consideration of the Governor.

" Signed on behalf and at the request of our brethren.

" JONATHAN MIFFLIN,
" ISRAEL PEMBERTON,
" SAMUEL PRESTON MOORE,
" ABRAM DAWES.

" 3d Eleventh Month, 1756."

The Governor sent the following reply to Israel
Pemberton :—

" SIR :—I have considered the address delivered me this morning, in behalf of a considerable number of the people called
Quakers, and am willing to receive such goods as they may put into
my hands for the use of the Indians, and deliver them along with the
Provincial present, in the same manner Mr. Morris did. I thank
the gentlemen for their kind offer of attending me at the Indian
conference, and shall be glad to see them at Easton.

" I am, sir, your very humble servant,

" WILLIAM DENNY."

It was now agreed by Friends, to purchase goods
and clothing, to the value of five hundred pounds, and
send the same to Easton, to be there distributed by the

committee in attendance, as they may deem necessary. Jeremiah Warder, Samuel Sansom, William Fisher, and Abel James, were appointed to purchase goods, and hire wagons, to send them to Easton. Charles Jones was authorized to buy liquors, and provisions, and send them with the goods. Joseph Richardson, Thomas Crosby, Daniel Williams, James Pemberton, Joshua Emlen, and Owen Jones, were to solicit subscriptions for defraying " the expenses of this business."

On the 4th of Eleventh Month, eighteen Friends met. It was announced at this meeting, that Captain New-castle, who had been seized with the small-pox, died on the 3d.

"Having first expressed his mind fully concerning his burial and the care of his widow, and nephew and niece, whom he called his children, which being committed to writing, and the Governor de-claring his approbation of the will being performed, it is therefore now agreed, that Kelly, the said Newcastle's nephew, be immediately clothed and lodged at John Hill's, and after the treaty is over, be put to school, to learn to read and write."

John Reynell, James Pemberton, Owen Jones, and Anthony Benezet, were appointed a committee, to take charge of Newcastle's burial.

"At a meeting of the committee, 19th Eleventh Month, 1756, present all but Anthony Morris and Jeremiah Elfreth. The mem-bers of the committee who attended the treaty at Easton, gave an account of their conduct and proceedings there, and of the agree-able issue of these conferences, &c., and as all the goods provided were not presented to the Indians, those brought back, are left under the care of Jeremiah Warder. After some further conversation relative to the business, agreed to meet again to-morrow afternoon, at three o'clock, at the Schoolhouse, and to invite to the said meeting, the Friends nominated to assist this committee in making an essay of rules, &c."

The following account, is given by some of the Trustees, who attended the late treaty with the Indians at Easton :—

"The Governor having on the 5th inst., in the morning, set out from Philadelphia with the Secretary, several of the Trustees and other Friends followed in the afternoon, and others the next day. At Samuel Dearies, about twenty miles from Easton, one of the Trustees (Israel Pemberton), accompanied by Charles Thomson, overtook the Governor, and were informed that on some intelligence sent by the Moravians from Bethlehem, of the Indians intending some mischief, the Governor had stopped until the Commissioners came up, and he had received an answer to a message he had sent to Colonel Weiser at Easton. The Governor was then informed that the commissioners had gone another road, and would probably that night reach John Chapman's, ten miles further on the way towards Easton, and that they intended likewise to go thither, not being apprehensive there was any danger from the Indians. The Secretary therefore wrote a letter to the commissioners, which was sent by a messenger, to meet them on the road. *   *   * The Governor having been delayed several days longer than was expected, Israel Pemberton and Charles Thomson concluded to go forward to Easton. About noon on the 7th they arrived there, and on the bank of the river before the ferry-house, were received by Teedyuscung, and about fifteen or sixteen of his people, with a hearty welcome. They were inquisitive about the Governor's coming, and being told he was on the road and would be here soon, they said they had been told so before and did not know how to believe it, but if Israel Pemberton said so, they would believe it, and upon being assured of its truth, they retired to their camp. In a short time, the Governor and Secretary came. Teedyuscung, two of the Six Nations Indians, and Israel Pemberton went to the Governor's lodgings to congratulate him on his arrival. In the evening, the Commissioners, and some of the Trustees arrived. Beds having been sent from Philadelphia, we were all more agreeably accommodated than at the former treaty. It soon appeared that our coming had relieved the Indians from a painful suspense, which the imprudent conduct and discourse of the people who had come hither from the Jerseys, and other parts of the country had increased, many of them having threatened to take this opportunity of being revenged on them. Some one hundred and sixty Indians (as we were informed), had prepared to leave Teogan (Tioga) for the treaty, but the night before setting out, they received a message from the northward, that some Indians at Mount Johnson, had heard from their brethren at Philadelphia, that the intention of the Government of Pennsylvania in inviting them to a treaty, was to get a number of them together and cut them off; that at or near Wyoming two messages of similar import had been received, so that many had been deterred from setting out, and scarce one-third of the number expected were come hither."   *   *   *   *

On the afternoon of the 8th, the conferences were opened. Teedyuscung first spoke, and the Governor briefly answered by way of introducing the business. The chief, believing that the Governor was disposed to "accommodate matters," sent a messenger to the Indians in the vicinity of Fort Allen, to invite them to join in the treaty. The Governor's Secretary, requested Charles Thomson to assist in taking minutes, which he complied with, and continued to do so, until the conclusion of the treaty.

The conference was renewed, about eleven o'clock on the morning of the 9th. The chief revived the memory of former treaties, and assured those assembled that he had sought to restore peace, and had told his people that the whites were seeking to revive the "ancient alliance and friendship, by a candid and ingenuous conduct." The Governor promised to reply the next day. The conference adjourned, and by invitation four members of the Association, dined with the Governor.

" 10th of Eleventh Month, 1756. This being the King's birthday, the Governor invited all the Friends here, and the Indians, to a public entertainment. Some of us wholly declined going, others attended, to prevent any exception being taken by the Governor, and to show ourselves heartily disposed to keep the Indians in a proper disposition to bring the treaty to the desired issue, our minds being more disposed to promote that, than to indulge in feasting. It being generally thought necessary to try to bring down the Indians remaining above, and the Governor, Commissioners, and all concerned having declared their approbation of the design, several Friends expressed their willingness to accompany Moses Tetamie, whom with two other Indians, Teedyuscung concluded to send. Just before they were to set out, he came to our lodgings, and taking I. Zane and Israel Pemberton into a private room, told them he had provided a string of wampum, and expected the Governor would send one, and desired the Quakers might add another, which three being tied together, he said he would send them to be delivered with his message. We told him we should cheerfully do it if the Governor approved, and Israel Pemberton went immediately to W. Logan, one of the Governor's Council, and desired he would let us know the Governor's pleasure. About this time, it was whispered that the Governor did not approve of Friends going, so that those who had proposed it, declined. We afterward learned that the Governor forbid our sending any wampum, but left our going to the discretion of Conrad Weiser, who, being consulted, approved it. Daniel Stanton, John Pemberton, and Benjamin Hooton being willing to go, application was made to the Secretary, for a pass or letter from the Governor to the Captain of Fort Allen, which he readily promised to prepare." Subsequently, but after considerable delay, "he delivered a letter, sealed and directed to Captain Ornt, and immediately the messengers and Friends with them set out. It was a cold, tempestuous time, yet they traveled all night. At an ordinary on the road to Fort Allen, they met with one of the captains of the party of Indians they were sent to, who was coming down to Teedyuscung. On being informed of their business, the captain agreed to return and to propose to his company their coming down to Easton. In the morning the party arrived at Fort Allen and were kindly received by Captain Ornt. There being no road from the fort to the Indian camp, and it being necessary to ford the river several times to get there, Friends remained at the fort, while Moses Tetamie and the Indians, went to the camp. In the evening, Moses returned, and stated they had met in council for several hours, and at last concluded to remain where they were, and would leave it to their Chief to attend the council fire, and they would agree to whatever he did. But that they might not appear ungrateful for so civil an invitation, and the kindness of Friends

who accompanied the messengers, one of their captains, with most
of his company, visited the fort the next morning, and after a conference with Friends, appeared free and open, and lost much of the
suspicion which they had discovered ; and after a handsome acknowledgment of this instance of regard to them, concluded to
send two of their company, to wait on the Friends back to Easton.
In the evening of the 10th, after dinner, divers Jersey people be-
haved with great impudence, many of them appearing outrageous
and very valiant, now they think without danger to themselves [to]
take advantage of Indians. One young man was so turbulent that
a writ was prepared to put him into custody."

11th of Eleventh Month. The Governor concluded
to defer proceeding to business, until the return of the
messengers sent to Fort Allen.

"Friends met together at our hired house, at the usual time of
our weekly meeting in Philadelphia, and were favored with a satisfactory evidence of the renewings of Divine regard toward us,
uniting us to each other, and encouraging us in the prosecution of
our business. At this meeting, we had the company of our Friends,
Christopher Wilson and John Hunt, from Great Britain, who came
hither yesterday out of Chester county, accompanied by several
Friends residing there."

12th of Eleventh Month. Moses Tetamie returned,
with the information that the Indians around Fort
Allen, would not attend the treaty, whereupon the
Governor concluded to proceed to business in the
afternoon. A warm debate, arose between the Secretary and Commissioners, about what should be said to
the Indians, the latter contending, that they should be
asked the cause of their disaffection, while the former
urged, that such a question was unnecessary, it being
evident they had been prevailed on by the French, to
"strike their old friends." The Commissioners, however, declared that the question had never been asked

the Indians officially, and Secretary Peters finally con-
sented, that they might be asked in a general way, why
they were dissatisfied; but that no direct query as to
whether the Proprietaries or their agents had wronged
them, would be allowed. As Israel Pemberton remarks :—

" Surely, if he (Peters) was assured that justice had always been
done to them, this must be a fair opportunity of a public testimony
of it, and the suspicions in the minds of many, be effectually removed.

" About half-past four o'clock, the Governor delivered his speech
to the Indians, and the joy which appeared in their countenances
cannot be expressed, on their hearing what the Governor said.
There has not for many years been a treaty, in which they have
given such full and repeated expressions of approbation by their
hearty, united '*yeho*' at the end of every sentence. On the
meeting breaking up, they hurried across the benches, to offer the
Governor their hands. One of them cried, 'O! he is a good man;
there is no evil in his heart.' Every one seemed pleased, that if
they have any complaints to make, the way is now so fairly opened
for their making them known, that the grounds of them may be
inquired into.

"In the evening, the three Friends returned from Fort Allen.
On their alighting, the sentinel informed them, they were desired to
wait on the Governor. After a tedious delay, they were admitted
to him, and upon giving him some account of their business, were
much surprised to hear him declare, that he was unacquainted with
their going, and disapproved it. They informed him, they had gone
with the full apprehension of its being with his privity, and with
no other view, than the promotion of the business in the manner
they thought he desired. At our lodgings, they were told by us,
that it was impossible the Governor should have been ignorant of
their going, as he had signed the pass for them ; but they declared,
that when Captain Ornt opened the paper at the fort, it was un-
signed, and as the captain thought it an accidental omission,
they were treated with kindness and civility. As the Governor
was quite ignorant of the care we had taken to be assured of his
consent, by applying for his letter or pass, and as there was danger

of interrupting the business, by a controversy with the Secretary to clear the matter up, it seems we were to lie under the imputation, of having willfully acted contrary to his direction. The Friends who performed this fatiguing journey, seemed however, so fully satisfied of having been in the discharge of their duty, that we endeavored to exercise patience and prudence."

13th of Eleventh Month. The conference re-opened, about noon. Teedyuscung freely expressed his mind, and alluded to the frauds practiced upon his people. Conrad Weiser, sought to evade the subject of frauds, and Secretary Peters, declined to take notes of what was said; but Charles Thomson, was requested by the Governor, to record all that passed, which, it is asserted, he did, with great precision. After adjournment, a few Friends dined, by invitation, with the Governor, who expressed his willingness to inquire into the matter of frauds more fully at a future time, but Benjamin Franklin, feared that a long postponement would be construed by the Indians as a—

"Denial or refusal of justice, and instanced the treaty at Albany, where they had complained of being deceived by promises so frequently, that they insisted on the Commissioners then present, being guarantees, for the faithful performance of some promises made by New Yorkers. What a reproach is this, to the Christian name! In what contempt must it be held by those heathen, when the professors of it cannot be believed?"

14th of Eleventh Month, First day. Moses Teta-mie called in the morning at "*Scull's*," where some of the Friends lodged, and gave them an account of the "Walking Purchase," as narrated to him by some of the older Indians—

"In what manner they thought the land was agreed to be walked, how far it was carried into execution in the first Proprietors' days, and the complaints the Indians had made, ever since the walk in 1737. He likewise explained the meaning of a paragraph in Teedyuscung's last speech, which seemed to be diversely understood, by which it appeared, that if the Governor had not in so explicit a manner called upon the Indians to tell the true cause of their uneasiness, they only should at present have wiped off the blood and cleared the way, and left the adjustment of land affairs, until next spring, when a greater number of Indians might be present." Some thirty or forty Friends, assembled this day for worship. C. Wilson and J. Hunt, had very acceptable service. There were present, also, all the commissioners, some Indians, and others. The Governor dined with Friends, at '*Vernon's,*' and in the afternoon attended church, where Secretary Peters, preached on r able of the unjust steward.'

"In the evening, some of our company, in conversation with William Parson (the Proprietary's agent at Easton), were informed by him of the particulars of Charles Brodhead's conduct, by which the truth of Teedyuscung's remarks about him is confirmed. It appears that the imprudence of the Minisink people, in sending him to the Indians, his abusive conduct among them, and his perfidy in afterwards secreting the messages they sent by him, for several weeks, gave the Indians cause to apprehend this government had determined to break with them. And it may not be easy yet to convince them of the contrary, if they should hear, that the then Governor, had rewarded him with a commission, which he still bears."

"15th of Eleventh Month. This morning, Secretary Peters came to the house where two of the trustees (*J. W. and A. J.) boarded, and asked for the latter, who came to him, and he immediately, in a confused manner, addressed him thus:—

"'You took some minutes at the last conference.' A. J. replied he had. The Secretary said, he wanted to see them. A. J. said they were not with him, but they were at a house close by, and he would fetch them. Peters replied, 'There is no occasion, for you can tell me how you understood what Teedyuscung said, respecting the English Government being greedy in the purchase of lands from the Indians, for Mr. Thomson has got it, that the Proprietaries were greedy in buying land, and had purchased of

those who had no right to sell, which was Mr. Franklin's interpre-
tation, to blacken the Proprietors and support a party : that the
Proprietaries could not be charged therewith, nor indeed had Teedyuscung said any such thing, and that the Proprietaries had always
been solicited by the Indians, to buy.' To which A. J. replied,
'That he had understood the Indians charged the Proprietaries,
as well as others, with unfairness, and that the Indians complained of the Proprietaries, in particular, about the very lands we
were on, being part of the walking purchase.' The Secretary
again repeated, that it was well known, that the Proprietaries had
never been greedy of the purchase of land, nor did the Indians
complain upon that account, except of the people of the Province.
He was then informed that the people had not pretended a right to
purchase of the Indians, and that the Walking Purchase was particularly complained of. He admitted then, that the '*walk*' could
not be vindicated. 'The Proprietaries always despised it,' he said,
'and it was unworthy of any government.' He was then asked
why the Proprietaries held this land under the Walking Purchase.
To which he answered, 'They have paid several times for it.' A
short time after this conversation, these two Trustees, with several
others, were in their chamber at an inn. Peters hurried up-stairs,
rudely opened the door of the room, and said, 'These practices
shall not be suffered. You shall be taken proper notice of. You
are putting things into the Indians' heads.' One Friend asked him,
civilly, to walk in. He said 'No,' shut the door, and hurried
down-stairs. They desired him to come back, and make good his
charge ; that we were innocent of it. But he refused, and went off
in a great passion, upon which they followed him, and insisted upon
knowing which of them he intended to charge, as they told him
they were each ready to declare their innocence of saying anything
to the Indians to the prejudice of any person. He replied to two
of them, after some further conversation, saying, 'It is not you. It
is an affront to your good understandings, to take it to yourselves.'
They told him they were equally persuaded of the innocence of
every Friend there, and insisted upon his going with them to any
Friends he suspected, and have the matter cleared up. Upon
which they went together to the house hired by Friends, where he
met with Teedyuscung, his interpreter, and several Friends. They
told him, that Teedyuscung came to them to communicate his
uneasiness, on account of the several threats which had been
given them, and that he was apprehensive some of his people

were gone, and more would go, by reason of the alarm occasioned last night.*

" The Secretary now declared he was fully satisfied that the Friends spoke truth, and that he had been misinformed. Thus his being unwilling that the Indians should be asked the cause of their uneasiness, and when they answered, his declining to minute what they said, and now denying that which more than twenty persons can readily prove they heard spoken by the interpreter ; these actions appear to indicate a fixed purpose, at all adventures, to confuse, misrepresent, and obstruct an honest, fair inquiry, in order to an amicable adjustment of the difficulties. For to what purpose can be the carping at one word? Is not the tenor of several paragraphs of the Indian's speech, a continued complaint against the unjust dealing of the Proprietaries and their agents? None but the Proprietors in this province have a right to buy land of the natives, and against whom do the Indians complain, but against the purchasers of land, unless we allow that they tacitly reflect on the Assembly, for consenting to a law confining the purchase of lands solely to the Proprietaries, and not having a guarantee of just and open dealing by them therein. There is indeed one complaint against the people,—that they hinder the Indians from getting a livelihood by hunting, this being their principal means of support, the right of which, they have seldom relinquished. So common is the practice of killing deer by people in the inner parts of the Province, that it is said, even in the present unsettled state of affairs, several wagons have been fitted out, and people come with them from Bucks county, and journey towards Fort Allen, on purpose to hunt, which is disagreeable to the Indians and dangerous to themselves. But by this, and other imprudences, the Indians have been driven from us, into the arms of the French. Another grievance constantly complained of in former treaties, which has alienated the Indians from us, is our suffering a set of *banditti*, under the name of *traders*, to go among them, and after debauching them with rum and whisky, cheat them of their skins. Without redressing these grievances, treaties and presents will not avail.

---

* On the night before, it had been rumored that a party of whites, intended to kill the Indians while they were asleep, and the imprudence of some, led to apprehensions of mischief, so that the Governor had ordered the camp to be doubly guarded, and all the boats near the town to be secured, to prevent people coming from New Jersey, as they had threatened to do. Several days before, a peddler was committed to jail, who had offered to furnish some of the soldiers with knives, and to join them in cutting the throats of the Indians—he engaging to destroy Tee-dyuscung.

"While the writer is employed in these notes, the Secretary and Commissioners, are disputing about what answer to make the Indians. The Secretary, it is said, is for taking no notice of complaints about lands, or for postponing their consideration. The Commissioners are for removing the cause immediately, if in our power, by asking what will satisfy them, and doing it; so that if they continue their hostilities, they will be left without excuse. This is at last agreed upon. The Secretary meets Israel Pemberton and professes much concern, for the unhappy difference occurring this morning between himself and some Friends, when Israel Pemberton tells him that if he had said as much to *him*, it would not have given the least offence ; shows him a part of the proposed answer to the Indians, which he was taking from the Governor to the Commissioners for review, before transcribing, and he is apparently quite friendly. Soon after this, the conferences were opened. The Governor spoke fully to the Indians, and informed them of the presents provided for them. It was remarkable that in the forepart of the Governor's speech this day, he attributed the attitude of the Indians, to *French influence.* If the part insisted on by the Commissioners had not been added, and notes been preserved of the complaints, it might afterwards have been said, that the Indians had no grievances against the Government about lands."

As some Friends had arrived from different parts of the country, a meeting of the Association was held in the evening, to which they were invited. The transactions of every day since the opening of the treaty, were read, and after some time profitably spent in correcting misapprehensions concerning the conduct and views of members of the Association, and the importance of being united in the prosecution of their work, some Friends, "who had hitherto been backward," decided to join the Association.

16th of Eleventh Month. Teedyuscung this morning returned his answer to the Governor, "by a metaphor of planting and tending Indian corn." He desired the removal of all obstructions to a durable peace, and said that as to the demand they should make for satisfaction in the purchase of lands, it must be referred to a future treaty, as the long continuance of frauds, had increased the damages, and many who were concerned in these matters, were not present. *He urged, that Friends might have liberty to examine into their complaints,* and asked for a written copy, of the minutes of the treaty. He asserted, that he had but two prisoners in his power, but he might be able to have more released with the assistance of the Governor. He then presented the Governor with some deerskins, who in turn, gave him the presents previously alluded to. The gifts provided by Friends, were distributed separately. And Israel Pemberton says:—

" It was a particular satisfaction to us to have them delivered in this way, that it might plainly appear, we did not present them with ammunition or anything of this kind, which we were charged with doing at the former treaty, when to conceal the smallness of the Provincial presents, ours were mixed with them, and delivered promiscuously."

17th of Eleventh Month. This day the conferences ended. " The Governor renewed his application about the prisoners, and condoled with them, on the death of several of their people, by the small-pox, at Philadelphia." (They had privately expressed their wonder, that this allusion to their deceased brethren had been so long omitted, which, according to their custom, would have been an early part of their business, if any of the whites had died among them.) Israel Pemberton proposed the delivery of " several hundred pieces of eight," to Teedyuscung, for the redemption of prisoners in the hands of the Indians, but Weiser seemed doubtful of its propriety, and stated, that some Mohawks would be intrusted with that service, whereupon Israel announced, the willingness of Friends to contribute liberally, to this laudable purpose.

Six Trustees waited upon the Governor, to attest their appreciation of his integrity and candor in these public transactions, who acknowledged their kindness, and expressed his gratification that Friends were present during the treaty. The secretary (Peters), in taking leave of Friends, hoped that any undue warmth which he had shown might be forgiven, and " Conrad Weiser, declared we had been of service in promoting the public interest, and hoped we would banish from our minds, all disagreeable thoughts concerning him."

" Teedyuscung, and most of his people, came down to the ferry-house and dined with us ; before parting with Isaac Zane and Israel Pemberton, he took them aside, and told them, that a few days before, he found what was said to him went to his heart, and brought tears into his eyes ; that he now found his heart affected in the same manner, and *his speaking being interrupted by a flood of tears,* after privately venting himself, he returned, and told them that in the course of this business, he had endeavored to turn in his mind, and look up to God for direction ; that when he was alone in the woods and destitute of every other counsellor, he found by doing so, he had the best direction ; that he hoped God would bless our endeavors, and wanted Friends to remember him. He followed us to the boat, and was so much affected, he could only by tears manifest his respect, which, as it appeared to be the effect of a Divine visitation to a savage barbarian, was a humbling scene, and excited reverent and thankful sentiments, in the minds of those immediately observing it."

Thus ends this interesting account of a memorable treaty, which, as previously stated, was read before a meeting of interested Friends, held 19th Eleventh Month, 1756. The conferences with the Indians on

that occasion, revealed to the Governor the important
fact, that they were smarting under the injustice practiced by Thomas and John Penn, or their authorized
agents, in the purchase of lands, and this open confession on their part, was owing to the confidence they
felt, that Friends present, would endeavor to rectify the
wrong committed. The old love for William Penn,
burned anew in their breasts for "*his children*," (as all
the Quakers were called,) which, while it awakened
envy and suspicion in the minds of some officials,
nevertheless gave a *status* to the "Friendly Association," whose aid had been so important.

On the 20th of Eleventh Month, the minutes of the
treaty at Easton, as prepared by Charles Thomson,
who was employed as a clerk, with the approval of the
Governor, were produced and read at a meeting of the
Association. It was—

"Agreed, that Israel Pemberton should write to Dr. John Fothergill, of London, informing him of our conduct and proceedings,
and send him a copy of these minutes.

"Agreed, that copies of all the deeds on record, for lands released
by the Indians to the Proprietaries, from the first settlement of this
Province, be obtained, and Israel Pemberton is appointed to apply
to the Master of the Rolls, for such as are in his office.

"S. P. Moore, Thomas Crosby, Daniel Williams, John Reynell,
Abel James, and Israel and James Pemberton, are desired to form
an essay of such rules as they may think necessary, &c., and they
agree to meet for that purpose on Second-day evening, next, at 5
o'clock.

"Adjourned to meet next Fourth-day evening, at 5 o'clock, at
the Schoolhouse.

"On the 24th Eleventh Month, most members of the committee
present. An essay of rules for regulating the trust, authority, and
duty of the Trustees and Treasurer, were now produced, read, considered, and recommitted, to be altered, explained, and amended.
Adjourned to meet on Seventh-day next, at 5 o'clock, in the Schoolhouse.

"On the 27th Eleventh Month, eleven of the committee met, and after considering sundry matters relative to the business under our care, adjourned till next Second-day, at 5 o'clock in the evening.

"On the 29th Eleventh Month, present all of both committees but five. Accounts were now brought in of sundry subscriptions lately made, and the names of subscribers, were added to the former list. The original subscription paper, containing most of the subscriptions, was now delivered to the Treasurer. Adjourned after other conversation on our business till to-morrow eve, at five.

"On the 30th Eleventh Month, present fifteen Friends. A further essay of the rules, was now produced and read. Agreed that the following proposals be made to the *General Meeting* to-morrow, viz.:—

"That the heads of the rules and articles, &c., only be agreed to *at present.*

"That the reducing them to a proper form and order, to become a public act, be afterwards perfected by the Trustees, and such of the members of this Association as may be chosen to take a bond from the Trustees and Treasurer.

"That after the said heads, &c., are agreed on, the Trustees may be chosen by ballot. That afterwards the persons be chosen to whom the Trustees and Treasurer may give bonds.

"That lastly, the time of our next *General Meeting* be agreed on. Adjourned.

"At a General Meeting of the contributors towards a fund for regaining and preserving peace with the Indians, in Friends' Great Meeting-house, in Philadelphia, the 1st of Twelfth Month, 1756. Present Anthony Morris, Jonathan Mifflin, Jeremiah Warder, John Reynell, Abel James, Jeremiah Elfreth, Joshua Emlen, William Fisher, Israel Pemberton, James Pemberton, Samuel Sansom, Thomas Say, Owen Jones, S. Preston Moore, Samuel Rhoades, Jacob Lewis, Richard Wistar, Thomas Crosby, Abram Dawes, Daniel Williams, of the Committee.

"Mathew Aspden, Anthony Benezet, David Bacon, Davis Bassett, William Brown, Jon'n Carmalt, John Cresson, William Clark, William Callender, Isaac Cathrall, John Drinker, Jr., John Drinker, Owen Evan, James Eddy, Benjamin Gibbs, Jr., Samuel Grisley, Isaac Greenleafe, Thomas Hallowell, Benjamin Hooton, John Hallowell, Joseph Hallowell, Joseph Jacob, Edward Jones, John Jones, merchant, William Lightfoot, Samuel Lewis, John Lyn, Joseph Lownes,

Joseph Marriot, Samuel Massey, Samuel Oldman, John Pemberton, Richard Parker, Joseph Richardson, Francis Richardson, Henry Shute, James Stackhouse, James Stephens, John Test, Peter Worrall, Robert Waln, Samuel Wetherill, Charles West, Jr., Isaac Zane.

" From Chester county—James Bartram, John Jacobs, George Miller, George Smedley, Nathan Taylor.

" From Germantown—Adam Gruber, Christopher Sower.

"From Towamensing—Caspar Krible, Christopher Shultz.

" From West Jersey—James Cooper, William Foster, James Whiteall.

"After an account given by the committee, of their proceedings soon after the late General Meeting, in applying to him* (their address to him, and his answer in writing being read), of their purchasing goods and sending them to Easton, and of their conduct there, the particulars of which are already entered in the minutes of the Trustees, the minutes of the late treaty at Easton were read, and afterwards the essay made by the committee of rules and articles for the regular management of the affairs of our Association, and for regulating the trust, authority, and duty of the Treasurer and Trustees, &c., was read. Then adjourned till 3 o'clock in the afternoon, to meet at the Schoolhouse and consider the same."

At the afternoon meeting, there were present, in addition to the above, Joseph Baker, John Care, Joseph Davis, Thomas Davis, Cadwalader Evans, David Dishler, Solomon Fussell, Joshua Fisher, Benjamin Mason, Joshua Pearson, Jacob Shoemaker, Jr., Joseph Saul, William Savery, James Bartram, George Miller, and Nathan Taylor, "besides several others from different parts of the country, not members of our society."

" The essay of the rules, &c., prepared by the committee, being now again read and considered, agreed the term or name of our society or company be " The Friendly Association for Regaining and Preserving Peace with the Indians by Pacific Measures."

---

* The Governor.

"Agreed, that the duty, &c., of the Treasurer be settled, pursuant to the proposals of the committee. The following Trustees were chosen by ballot, viz.:—Israel Pemberton, Jonathan Mifflin, Jeremiah Warder, Isaac Zane, Abram Dawes, Benjamin Lightfoot, Abel James, George Miller, James Pemberton, Thomas Say, William Callender, Joseph Richardson, Owen Jones, Joseph Morris, Richard Wistar, William Fisher.

"Agreed, that the duty, &c., of the Trustees, be regulated agreeable to the proposals of the committee.

"Agreed, that the said Trustees, shall reduce the rules and articles aforesaid to proper order, with a suitable preamble, to be considered at our next meeting.

"It is recommended to all such members of this Association who can conveniently pay the sums they have respectively subscribed, to do it speedily to the Treasurer, and others, to give their bonds payable to him with interest, agreeable to the terms of their subscription.

"Thomas Crosby, Jeremiah Elfreth, Samuel Preston Moore, Charles Jones, Daniel Williams, Samuel Rhoades, Jacob Lewis, Hugh Roberts, Peter Worrall, Isaac Greenleafe, John Armitt, Joshua Emlen, Samuel Sansom, Jacob Shoemaker, Jr., David Bacon, and Joshua Howell, are appointed to take the bonds from the Trustees.

"Adjourned till 19th Fourth Month next, unless the Trustees think proper to call a General Meeting sooner."

"At a General Meeting of the members of the Association for Regaining and Preserving Peace with the Indians, the First day of the Twelfth Month, 1756, the following articles or rules were agreed on, viz. :—

"That the Treasurer of this Association, shall enter into an obligation unto the Trustees, with one surety in double the value that doth or may probably come into his hands, during the continuation of his office, conditioned that he will once in three months, or oftener if required, render his account to the said Trustees, and well and truly account, adjust, and settle with them, when required, for and concerning all moneys that are or shall come into his hands belonging to the members of this Association, and pay all such sums unto such person, or persons, or for such services as a board of Trustees for the time being, shall order and appoint, and not otherwise ; and that he will, at the expiration of his office, well and truly deliver up and pay the balance of the money then remaining in his hands, together with the books of accounts concerning the same, and all the bonds, papers, and writings, and all other effects and matters in his keeping belonging to this Association, to his successor in the said office, without any deduction, defalcation, or abatement for, or on account of commissions or wages, for executing the said trust; and that he will faithfully do and execute, all other things as Treasurer, to the members of this Association. And if the present Treasurer, or any one hereafter chosen Treasurer, shall be rendered incapable, or neglect his office or duty, the Trustees for the time being, are hereby empowered to displace him from the said office or trust, and the Trustees causing their Clerk to make a minute for that purpose, explaining their reasons for displacing him, he shall thereupon and thenceforth, cease to be Treasurer, and shall, upon notice thereof, adjust and settle with the Trustees, and pay and deliver the money, books, writings, accounts, and all other effects whatsoever in his hands, belonging to this Association, to such person or persons as the Trustees shall order or appoint; and in that case, and also if the Treasurer shall depart this life, the Trustees shall nominate another member of this Association, but not of their own number, to be Treasurer, until the next General Meeting of the members of the Association.

" That the Trustees shall have the power of disposing of all moneys paid by members to the Treasurer, for purchasing goods to be presented to the Indians at the times of treaties with them, or at any other time, when it shall be deemed necessary and conducive to the public interest, and with the approval or consent of the Government under which we live; or for providing for the maintenance of such Indian children as they may think proper to take under their care, to educate in the principles of the Christian religion, and to qualify them for interpreters, and in that, or some other station, to become more serviceable to themselves and the Government.

" Likewise, that the said Trustees shall have power to call general meetings, as often as they think necessary, and be enjoined to keep minutes of all articles, rules, and agreements, as shall be agreed on in such meetings, and take care that all such rules and orders be duly observed and faithfully executed. And for the more orderly execution of their trust, the Trustees are to meet at least once a month, and as much oftener as the business of the Association may require, at such place, and on such day or days, as they may think most convenient, to examine and settle accounts with the Treasurer from time to time, and to confer and conclude concerning the matters hereby committed to them ; and they shall cause fair minutes of their proceedings, to be kept by their Clark, in a book provided for that purpose. In every of which meetings of the Trustees, ten at least shall be a quorum, capable to confer, &c., and whatsoever nine of them shall agree and conclude upon, shall be deemed and taken as the resolution of the Trustees for the time, and accordingly entered in the minutes, to which minutes, and also to the Treasurer's accounts, all persons concerned, shall have free recourse at all seasonable times.

" And for the more general satisfaction of all concerned, the Trustees are enjoined, before any Indian treaty (if time will permit), to call a General Meeting of all the members of the Association ; or if any sixteen members subscribing to the amount of two hundred pounds, shall at any other time desire a General Meeting, and notify their desire in writing to the Trustees, they shall call one.

" We likewise agree, that no person shall be chosen a Trustee unless he be a member in unity with the people called Quakers, and hath contributed at least ten pounds to the common fund of this Association ; and that no person shall be allowed to vote for Trustees at the general meetings, who has not contributed at least forty shillings. If any person chosen as Trustee, shall refuse or neglect to act, or shall be absent from three successive monthly meetings of the Trustees ; or if he shall be confined by sickness, or otherwise be rendered incapable of discharging the trust, or shall die, the rest of the Trustees shall proceed in their trust without him, or if they think fit, shall nominate another, until the next ensuing election, or other General Meeting.

" That the accounts of the Treasurer, and the minutes of the said Trustees, be settled, at the time of the annual election, or as much oftener as is required by a General Meeting, and be submitted to the examination of such committee, as the General Meeting may appoint.

" The present Treasurer and Trustees, this day chosen to serve until 19th of Fourth Month next, on which day, between the hours of ten in the morning and four in the afternoon, at the Public-schoolhouse in Philadelphia, a new choice to be made, and every year after on the same day, of which the Trustees are to give general notice, at least six days before. The Trustees are to give bond to sixteen others of the subscribers, in such sum as the last mentioned sixteen may require, conditioned that they will well and truly account for the disposition of all sums of money intrusted to them, and produce proper vouchers, to prove that no part has been applied to their own use, but to the uses and purposes intended by this Association.

"And lastly, that all money remaining in stock at the end of ten years, if a peace be concluded and the services proposed by this Association be answered, may be equally divided among the contributors, in proportion to each of their subscriptions, unless at the General Meeting it shall be otherwise ordered."

At a meeting of Trustees and Treasurer, held in the Schoolhouse, 4th of Twelfth Month, 1756.

"By the minutes of the General Meeting of the members of the Association, &c., now produced and read, it appears that on the Second day of last month, John Reynell was chosen Treasurer, and that on the first instant, the following sixteen Trustees were chosen by ballot, viz.:—Israel Pemberton, Jonathan Mifflin, Jeremiah Warder, Isaac Zane, Abram Dawes, Benjamin Lightfoot, Abel James, George Miller, James Pemberton, Thomas Say, William Callender, Joseph Richardson, Owen Jones, Joseph Morris, Richard Wistar, and William Fisher. And the Treasurer, and all the Trustees except Benjamin Lightfoot, Joseph Morris, and William Fisher, now attended, and unanimously agree to meet on the Third-day of the first week in every month, at three o'clock in the afternoon, and as much oftener as business may require; and that every member who lives in Town, and neglects to attend, shall pay a fine of two shillings for being wholly absent from such meetings, or one shilling for not attending punctually at the time appointed, which is to be determined by the State-House clock, *if it goes*; if not, by the watch of the oldest member present. And that the Clerk shall send written notices of all occasional meetings, at least six hours beforehand, to such Trustees who may not be present when such meetings are agreed on. Jonathan Mifflin, Jeremiah Warder, Isaac Zane, and Richard Wistar, with the Clerk, are desired to be a committee for such lesser services, as may occur between our monthly meetings, and if they judge at any time there is occasion for calling all the Trustees together, they are desired to send written notices to them signed by the Clerk. William Callender, Joseph Richardson, Owen Jones, James and Israel Pemberton, with the Treasurer, are appointed to get proper bonds drawn, one to be executed by the Treasurer, another by the Trustees, pursuant to the rules of the last General Meeting; and likewise to get the minutes of the General Meeting, and of the former committee of Trustees, revised, in order to be fairly entered in a book. Abel James, is desired to act as Clerk of this Association, until the next election of Trustees, and to collect all the accounts of money advanced, or goods supplied, by any of the contributors, in order to make a general adjustment of all accounts to the present time, that they may be paid and discharged, as soon as the Treasurer receives money sufficient for that purpose.

"Agreed that all the Trustees in Town meet again on Second-day next, at four o'clock in the afternoon, at the Schoolhouse, of which the Clerk is to give notice to the two Trustees who live in Town and are not now present."

On the 6th of Twelfth Month, at a meeting of Trustees, drafts of bonds were produced, which, after some amendments, were approved, and the committee presenting them, were authorized to get them transcribed to be laid before the next meeting.

" In consideration of Moses Tatamy's services at the late treaty, the standing committee are desired to give him the sum of five pounds, as a token of our regard for him.

"Joseph Morris and William Fisher, are desired to prepare and bring to our next meeting, essays of the three following drafts, viz.:—

"An obligation for each of the contributors of this society to execute, for the payment of their several subscriptions.

"A certificate for the Treasurer to sign and deliver each of those who have given forty shillings or upwards, upon their giving the aforesaid obligation, or paying the money they have subscribed, that they have given such a sum and are members of this Association. (See Appendix.)

"A proper subscription paper for future contributors to sign."

" 9th of Twelfth Month. The bonds to be signed by the Treasurer and Trustees, were read and approved. It was unanimously agreed, that two thousand pounds should be the penalty attached thereto. John Reynell, (Treasurer,) and John Pemberton, executed the former. All the Trustees present executed the latter, and then it was left in the care of Alexander Seaton, one of the witnesses, for the other five Trustees, (not present) to execute, and when done to be put in the hands of John Armitt, the Clerk first copying it with the Treasurer's bond on the minutes." (See Appendix.)

An essay of the three drafts previously alluded to, were presented and read, and after amendments, approved.

"The Clerk is desired to copy them fair, and with Jonathan Mifflin to have printed three hundred of the obligations, five hundred of the certificates, and one hundred of the subscription papers, and deliver the same to the Treasurer.

"William Callender and William Fisher, are appointed a committee on accounts, until another is chosen, and are desired to examine those already brought in, and report thereon.

"A considerable sum of money being already expended, and many debts contracted in the business of this Association, which ought to be discharged, it is now agreed that the Treasurer abate the interest due, on such subscriptions as may be paid him on or before the first day of next month. Adjourned."

13th of Twelfth Month. Agreed at this meeting, that "for the future, each member leaving the meeting before the minutes are read, and the time of adjournment agreed on, shall pay a fine of one shilling. Adjourned."

20th of Twelfth Month. The Clerk reported that the requisite number of obligations, certificates, and subscription papers, had been printed and handed to the Treasurer.

"The standing committee, acquainted the Trustees, that Joseph Peepys desires we would take his wife's son, named James, aged about seventeen years, and put him an apprentice to such place and trade as we may approve, for four years, between this and next spring ; the parents and the lad prefer a wheelwright trade. All which, is to remain under the notice of this board ; and the standing committee is desired to put and keep him at school. Adjourned to meet at Alexander Seaton's, on Sixth-day next, at five o'clock in the evening."

"24th of Twelfth Month. Nine members present. The Clerk is desired to notify Benjamin Lightfoot, that he is chosen a Trustee, and that his attendance is desired. There not being members of this board met, sufficient to proceed on business, we adjourned to meet at our next monthly meeting."

This Christmas eve meeting of the Trustees of the Friendly Association, ended their labors for 1756. Several large sums of money are mentioned in the book of minutes, as having been subscribed during this year, but the writer has no data, from which the precise amount can now be ascertained. It is evident, from papers in his possession, that active efforts were made by members of the Association, to collect funds from Friends throughout the limits of this Yearly Meeting.

The following committees were appointed to canvass the city:—

Jonathan Mifflin and Charles Jones, to call upon Friends residing within the following limits:—" From the North side of Chestnut street, to the South side of High street."

Joseph Richardson and Joseph Morris, "from the South side of Walnut street, to the South street."

John Reynell, Owen Jones, and James Pemberton, "from the North side of Walnut, to the South side of Chestnut street."

Jeremiah Elfreth, Joshua Emlen, Thomas Say, Samuel Sansom, and Abel James, "from the North side of Arch street, to the North Ward."

William Fisher, Jeremiah Warder, and Israel Pemberton, "from the North side of High street, to the South side of Arch street."

The aggregate amount subscribed by Gwynedd Friends this year, was one hundred and sixty-three pounds sixteen shillings, the names of the thirty-seven contributors, being as follows:—John Ambler, Joseph Ambler, Sr., Joseph Ambler, Jr., Robert Davies, Abraham Evans, Thomas Evans, Thomas Evans, Jr., Owen Evans, John Edwards, Robert Edwards, Thomas Foulke, William Foulke, John Forman, Hugh Griffith, Amos Griffith, Edward Hughes, Ellis Hughes, Isaac Jones, John Jones, Jesse Jones, Hugh Jones, Robert Jones, Jacob Kastner, Abraham Lukens, Enos Lewis, Garret Peters, Robert Roberts, John Roberts, John Roberts, Jr., Eldad Robets, Jonathan Robeson, Jr., George Shoemaker, Richard Thomas, John Thomas, John Williams, Daniel Williams, Abram Waggoner.

Providence monthly meeting, furnished one hundred and seventeen pounds five shillings, distributed amongst the following twenty-seven Friends:—James Bartram, John Calvert, Cadwallader Evans, Robert Evans, John Fairlamb, William Fell, Richard Gorman, John Heacock, Henry Howard, Isaac Howell, George Miller, John Minshall, Thomas Minshall, Robert Pennell, Samuel Parks, James Pennell, William Pennell, Jr., George Smedley, Joshua Smedley, James Sharpless, Samuel Sharpless, Peter Taylor, Nathan Taylor, Jonathan Vernon, Moses Vernon, Philip Yarnall, Nathan Yarnall.

The following twenty-three Friends, from Richland township, Bucks county, Pennsylvania, contributed one hundred pounds and fifteen shillings:—Thomas Adamson, Robert Ashton, Thomas Blackledge, Jr., Joseph Dennis, William Edwards, Samuel Foulke, Theophilus Foulke, Thomas Foulke, John Foulke, William Heacock, Lewis Lewis, Morris Morris, Robert Penrose, Thomas Roberts, Abel Roberts, Edward Roberts, Nathan Roberts, Richard Roberts, David Roberts, Samuel Shaw, Edward Thomas, John Thomas, Thomas Thomas.

Twenty-one Kennett Friends, under date of Seventh Month 22d, 1756, agree to pay to John Reynell, Treasurer, within twelve months, eighty-four pounds five shillings. Their names are as follows:—Daniel Bailey, Joel Bailey, Thomas Carleton, William Harvey, David Heyes, Thomas Harlan, Amos Hope, Amos Harry, Jacob Janney, Samuel Levis, Elizabeth Levis, William Levis, Isaac Mendenhall, Benjamin Mendenhall, Ruth Mendenhall, Ann Mendenhall, Daniel Nichols, Caleb Peirce, Thomas Temple, James Wickersham, Jacob Way.

The Association received aid, also, from the "Swing-felders," as appears from the following subscription paper:—

" It is the will of the within subscribers, that it may be known that they are a few families of a dispersed people in Silesia, who have always, under God's blessing, maintained themselves by the labors of their hands only, and have been forced to leave their estates behind in Silesia, on account of their confession, and who have already here, partly suffered by the incursions of the Indians, in relieving their poor distressed neighbors. Therefore, they hope that their contribution, small as it is, will not be contempted, for it may well be compared with the two mites which the poor widow in Evangelio cast in, for they have cast in their living. Nevertheless, they do it with cheerfulness, and delight to be assisting in the intended salutary endeavors, as also they are ready to testify their true loyalty to the King and Government to which they have submitted.

" KNOW ALL MEN BY THESE PRESENTS, That whereas, some of the principal members of the people called Quakers, within this Province of Pennsylvania, do intend to raise a considerable sum of money by way of a public and voluntary subscription, to lay a fund in order to be thereby enabled to do some satisfaction to those Indians who have already done terrible damage and disturbances to the frontier inhabitants of this Province, and therewith if possible to procure a peace to this country ; and as the said members have also communicated their said scheme to us, the hereunto subscribers, as late emigrants of Silesia, and desired of us to assist them in the above-mentioned purpose:—

"So know ye, therefore, that in consequence thereof, we, whose names are hereunto subscribed, do, in the name of God, hereby voluntarily, and of our own free-will and accord, promise to pay and contribute to the above said fund, which is to be employed to so salutary an end, consistent with the Gospel of our Saviour, and with the Principles of the Doctrine we profess, every one of us, all the respective sums of money as every one shall hereby promise and subscribe, on or before the twenty-seventh day of November next ensuing, after the date hereof, unto Caspar Kriebel and Christopher Shultze, as this day by us chosen and appointed Trustees for the term of two years from hence next ensuing, either in ready payment, or in case of non-payment, every one of us shall be at liberty to keep the principal sum in his hands, and to pay the interest for the same after the said twenty-seventh day of November next. To the true and punctual payment whereof, we do hereby oblidge and bind our heirs, executors, and administrators, and every of us and them, in the penalty of double the sum, as every one hereunto shall subscribe, firmly by these presents.

"In witness and confirmation, and for the true performance whereof, we have hereunto set our hands, together with the respective sums of money, as every one hereby promises to pay and contribute, to the purpose above mentioned.

"Done at Lower Salford township, in the county of Philadelphia, on this thirteenth day of November, Annoque Domini 1756."

The following forty-three names are attached to this document, and the aggregate amount of money subscribed was two hundred and six pounds:—

George Anders, George Bribel, George Drescher, Christopher Drescher, Ruides Estat, George Geydrich, Balthaser Geydrich, Hans Christopher Gubner, George Hoffman, Christopher Hubner, David Hubner, George Hubner, Casper Heydricq, Melchior Hartranft, Christr. Hoffman, Balthaser Hoffman, Christoper Jackel, Abraham Jackel, Baltzer Jackel, Caspar Kribel, Balthazer Krauss, Christoper Kribel, Melchor Kribel, Christoper

Krause, Melchor Meister, Christoper Milpem, David Meschter, Christr. Naumas, Christopher Reinwalt, Christr. Reinhald, Melchior Scholtz, George Scholtz, Gregorius Scholtz, David Scholtz, George Scholtz (2d), Christopher Scholtz, Caspar Seibt, Johannes Tackel, Christoper Tackel, Maria Tackerlen, Christopher Wagner, Hans Wiegner, Melchior Wiegner.

There are no other subscription papers for the year 1756, in the possession of the writer; but that a large amount of money was poured into the treasury of the Association, from peace-loving people, there can be no doubt.

From the "minute-book" it appears, that the first meeting of Trustees of the Association in the year 1757, was held on the fourth day of First Month, at the residence of Alexander Seaton ; present all the board but two. The committee appointed to inquire into the amounts due by the Association, made report, that there was owing, four hundred and seventy-four pounds eight shillings and six pence, principally to members of the Association, who had made liberal advances during the times of treaties, &c. Orders were drawn on the Treasurer, for the payment of the several sums, "when in cash." It was also ordered at this meeting, that the Treasurer continue to receive contributors' subscriptions "without interest, until the first of next month."

Captain George Croghan, deputy agent of Indian affairs for the Northern District, was at this time in Philadelphia, having been commissioned by General Johnson (superintendent of Indian affairs), to visit the Delawares and Shawnese, and inquire into the causes of their alienation. This fact was announced at the meeting of the Association, and four Friends were appointed to confer " with Captain Croghan, the Speaker of the Assembly, the Commissioners, or any others concerned in the Government, that they may find necessary, in order to demonstrate our readiness to join in promoting so good a design, by contributing our assistance, with a sum of money or otherwise, as occasion may require. Also, to apply to the Secretary and the keepers of the other records, for any minutes of the Governor and Council relative to Indian affairs, or for copies of any Indian deeds, &c. Adjourned."

8th of First Month, 1757. At a meeting held this date at A. Seaton's, the above committee reported, that Croghan had the sanction of the Governor and Assembly, to send messengers to the Indians on the Ohio, and invite them to a conference; and they recommend that the Association contribute funds towards this object. Accordingly, Croghan was supplied with one hundred pounds, and the Trustees "being informed that the *public treasury of this province is much exhausted*, it was agreed that out of the money now in the hands of John Reynell, our Treasurer, there be advanced and paid to Isaac Norris, Esq., Speaker of the House of Assembly, one hundred pounds, to defray the expenses which the Assembly have agreed to pay towards sending messengers, &c. to the Shawnees and Delaware Indians, living on the Susquehanna, and the Treasurer is desired to take the receipt of the Speaker, to be repaid *when there may be cash in the Provincial treasury*."

At a meeting held on the 11th of First Month, at A. Seaton's, Israel Pemberton read to the board, copies of the following messages sent by Captain Croghan :—

"BRETHREN, THE DELAWARES AT TEOGA, AND ON ALL THE BRANCHES OF SUSQUEHANNA :—Brother Teedyuscung, when I came here from Sir William Johnson, your brother Onas told me you had promised him another meeting in the spring, in order to settle all the differences subsisting between you and your brethren, the English, and as your brother, Sir William Johnson, has ordered me to assist at that meeting, and help to see matters reconciled, and justice done you, I desire you, by this belt of wampum, in the name of Sir William Johnson, your brother Onas, and the descendants of the first settlers who came over with your ancient brother, William Penn, to use your utmost endeavors to bring down all your people, and as many of your uncles, the Six Nations, who live among you, as will be necessary to accomplish this good work you began at Easton; and I promise you, in the name of Sir William Johnson, whom the great King of England, your father and his master, has ordered to take care of all the Indians in this part of America, that I will see justice done you." [A belt.]

" To the Chiefs of the Shawnese, Nanticokes, and Six Nations:

"BRETHREN OF SHAWNESE, NANTICOKES, AND SIX NATIONS, LIVING AT OTSANINGO AND DIAHOGO:—I came here about a month ago from Sir William Johnson, who is charged with the care of all the Indians in this part of America, by the great King of England, your father, and his master. On my arrival here, your brother Onas, showed me a copy of the conference he had with you at Easton, where I find you agreed to have another meeting in the spring, in order to settle all difference subsisting between you and your brethren, the English, and brighten the ancient chain of friendship, which has lately contracted some rust.

"And as your brother, Sir William Johnson, sent me here to inquire into the causes of the difference subsisting between you and your brethren, the English, in these parts, I promise you, in his name, that I will do everything in my power to settle the differences between you, and see full satisfaction made you for any injustice you have received; and that this meeting may be the more general and for the better settling all differences, I call a few of your chief men to meet me at John Harris', to consult on measures for bringing to this general meeting some of the chiefs of our brethren from Ohio, in order once more to brighten the ancient chain of friendship. In confirmation of which, I send you this belt of wampum in the name of Sir William Johnson, your brother Onas, and the descendants of the first settlers, who came here with your ancient brother William Penn, with whom you begun this good work at Easton this fall past." [A belt.]

A message of similar import was to be forwarded by messengers from Conestogo, to the Indians in the vicinity of Venango. No further business appearing, Friends adjourned.

At a meeting held at A. Seaton's, on the 25th of First Month—

"Israel Pemberton and William Callender, two of the committee appointed on the 4th instant, to apply to Richard Peters, Secretary, and the other keepers of the records of this Province, now report, that they had obtained from the Master of the Rolls copies of several deeds ; and that they applied to the said Secretary on the 20th instant, for liberty to search and copy any minutes of the Governor and Council of this Province relative to Indian affairs, which application the Secretary desired they would commit to writing, which was accordingly done on the 21st instant, and is as follows :—

"' PHILADELPHIA, 21st of First Month, 1757.

"'*Friend Peters* :—Pursuant to thy proposal, we now repeat in writing what we yesterday desired, which is that we may have the opportunity of searching the minutes of the Governor and Council, to satisfy ourselves and our friends, by whom we are deputed, of the true state of the Indian claims on the lands in this Province.

"'Our engagement in this inquiry, is with the view of promoting an amicable settlement of these matters, which we are desirous may be done in a manner conducive of the interest of the Proprietaries, as well as ourselves and fellow-subjects, in order to which we have raised a considerable fund, which we shall cheerfully contribute towards this purpose, if we are not prevented by those whose duty and interest, should engage them to promote this design.   An apprehension of the difficulties which may probably arise between the Proprietaries and the representatives of the people, in adjusting the quotas of expense which will attend a final settlement with the Indians, hath induced us to be prepared to contribute thereto, in order speedily to regain their friendship and that good understanding which hath unhappily been interrupted ; and as we find, by the express terms of our original deed, the Proprietaries are obliged to clear the lands of all titles, claims, or demands of the natives, we apprehend we have a right to be satisfied whether and how this hath been done, and, if we can, at the next treaty inform the Indians that agreeable to their desires at the last, we have had full opportunity of searching into the grounds of their complaints, and that we find they are under misapprehensions therein (which we have reason to believe is the case in some particulars), we are in hopes of being instrumental to engage them the more readily to comply with such measures as may be then proposed, for an amicable settlement of all differences between them and this Government, which is what we sincerely desire.

"'We are thy friends,

"'WILLIAM CALLENDER,
"'ISRAEL PEMBERTON.

"'To Richard Peters, Secretary of the Province of Pennsylvania.'"

To which the Secretary sent the following answer:—

"Gentlemen:—I laid your application with regard to the inspection of the council books, before his honor, the Governor, and in answer thereto, I am commanded to acquaint you, that as these books contain the most important affairs of government, many of which require the greatest secrecy, he cannot allow the perusal of them, to any but those concerned in the administration; and further, that he looks upon the transacting of business with the Indians in this Province, to be a matter so entirely pertaining to himself, that he cannot permit any but such as are immediately empowered by the King's authority, or by his own, to treat with or intermeddle in the affairs of that people. Nevertheless, if it be conceived that anything is contained in them inutes of Council, that does or may concern the right, or property of any person what soever, such person, by a proper application, and by particularly pointing it out, may be furnished with a copy of it. I am, gentlemen, your most humble servant,

"RICHARD PETERS.

"To Mr. William Callender and Mr. Israel Pemberton."

The committee also reported, that upon the receipt of this answer, they told the Secretary they had no wish to inspect the minutes of modern date, but only those, pertaining to matters long since transpired. After some consideration, the committee was continued, and they were urged to "acquaint the Speaker of the Assembly, and any other members or other persons concerned in the Government, with our proceedings herein, and report thereon to our next meeting." Then adjourned.

On the 2d of Second Month, the Trustees—all except five—met at Alexander Seaton's, when the propriety of publishing the minutes of the late treaties, &c. was considered, as a desire therefor had been expressed by some of the contributors. A committee was appointed to "get the minutes ready for the press, and to ascertain the cost of printing, unless, upon consultation with the Speaker of Assembly, the project should be disapproved by him, or others in authority, or that said minutes are to be printed by order of the Governor." Adjourned.

On the 8th of Second Month, the committee reported that the " House " have ordered " the minutes to be forthwith printed for the public good." The need of cash " to answer the demands upon the Treasurer " being discussed, he was " authorized to continue to receive any subscriptions paid him, on or before the 1st of Fourth Month next ensuing, without interest."

22d of Second Month. There being no quorum present, the meeting adjourned.

1st of Third Month. At a meeting held this day, it was announced that another treaty with the Indians was contemplated, and a committee of five was appointed to make out a list of goods most suitable to be presented to the natives, and to inquire the cost of them. No further business.

On the 8th of Third Month, the committee presented to the meeting a list of goods, and were continued.

15th of Third Month. The committee on accounts reported, that there was due to sundry members of the Association, for advances made, the sum of two hundred and thirty-two pounds nine shillings half-penny, and orders were drawn on the Treasurer, for one hundred and seventy-two pounds nine shillings half-penny, in part payment of the same.

A committee was appointed " to get an estimate of the cost of a parcel of silver medals, suitable to be presented to the Indians, and report the devices proposed, with the different expenses of each kind, at our next meeting; also, the cost of a number of silver armplates, wrist bands, &c."

22d of Third Month. The committee on medals produced a device which was approved, and they were continued.

"At an occasional meeting of most of the Trustees and Treasurer, on the 17th instant, it being notified that the Earl of Louden, Commander-in-Chief of the King's forces in America, since his coming to this city, had, in conversation with Richard Wistar, signified he had been informed of Friends being concerned in measures taken for restoring peace with the Indians; and it appearing that some part of our conduct therein had been misrepresented to him, Richard Wistar, Israel Pemberton, William Callender, and Owen Jones were then desired to wait upon him. They now report, they have have had the opportunity of a full and free conference with him, which they apprehend tended to his satisfaction, having truly informed him of our past conduct, and our further intentions as an Association. They also delivered him copies of our articles, and several papers respecting our proceedings, and as we are now informed there is a large number of Indians come within the settled parts of Lancaster county, and a treaty is soon to be held under the direction of Captain Croghan, Jeremiah Warder and Israel Pemberton, are appointed to confer with him on the occasion, and when they find it necessary, to call a meeting of all the Trustees and Treasurer." Then adjourned.

On the 29th of 3d Month, no quorum being present, the meeting adjourned.
On the 15th of 4th Month, present at A. Seaton's all the Trustees except four.

"A memorandum of the last words of Captain Newcastle, (lately deceased) was brought to this board by Isaac Zane, and is as follows:—

" 'MY GOOD FRIEND AND BROTHER GOVERNOR :—My two cousins shall have that fifty pounds given them, when I am dead. Betty shall live with Isaac Zane so long as she lives, and the boy with Joseph Peepy, and he must be good to him. My wife must go to her friends, from whence she came. All my friends must be kind to that woman ; (pointing to a Mohawk woman). I must be buried with my friends, the Quakers, when I am dead.

" 'These words wrote by John Hill, joiner, November 4th, 1756.'

" We hear, the sum of fifty pounds before mentioned, was claimed by Captain Newcastle for services done this Province, and our present Governor, William Denny, Esq., having given expectation of the payment thereof in behalf of this Government ;—

" Therefore, Jonathan Mifflin, Israel Pemberton, and Isaac Zane, are desired to use their endeavors to secure the payment of said sum, and place it out at interest for the benefit of the said Captain Newcastle's surviving niece."

The Treasurer was authorized to receive subscriptions without interest, until the 19th instant.

" George Croghan having applied to Israel Pemberton, for the sum of one hundred and fifty pounds, upon his draft on General Johnson (superintendent of Indian affairs), to defray the charge of bringing in and supplying a number of Indians who are come into Lancaster county, in consequence of the messages sent them last fall and winter, to hold a treaty for peace with the Government, and it not being convenient to call a meeting of the Trustees aforesaid, the money being immediately wanted, said Israel Pemberton furnished him with it, on his draft on General Johnson, which this board approves of, as it may answer a good purpose in promoting the work of peace.

"'Therefore, the Trustees unanimously agree, that the Treasurer do pay Israel Pemberton the said sum of one hundred and fifty pounds, and an order is accordingly drawn, dated this day, on the Treasurer in favor of Israel Pemberton, and when the draft is paid, Israel Pemberton is to repay the same to our Treasurer.

"Israel Pemberton produced his account of sundry disbursements for this Association, which was referred to the committee on accounts. Then adjourned."

At a meeting on the 8th of Fourth Month, several letters were read from George Croghan, dated Lancaster, containing information as to the number of Indians there assembled, &c., which led to the appointment of a committee "to wait upon the Commissioners and learn what provision they are making for clothing the Indians lately arrived at Lancaster, and for the presents, against the treaty, &c., and to offer our assistance, if it appears to be necessary." Adjourned.

12th of Fourth Month. Isaac Zane produced his account of disbursements, which was referred to the appropriate committee. The Clerk was desired to copy all the accounts "in the order they were brought in, in a book for the inspection of contributors, and he and Israel Pemberton are to collect and revise the late minutes of the Association, and copy them fair." The Friends selected to wait upon the Commissioners, reported that "they are making provision against the treaty, by order of the Assembly." Adjourned.

15th of Fourth Month. Sundry accounts were presented and referred. The Clerk reported that notices had been sent to country contributors, and the Trustees agreed to notify those in the city, "to meet on Third-day next, to make a new choice of Treasurer and

Trustees." "Adjourned till 5 o'clock next Second-day evening."*
18th of Fourth Month. The committee on accounts, reported the indebtedness of the Association to be two hundred and ninety-nine pounds ten pence half-penny, and orders were drawn on the Treasurer for the said sum.

Joseph Richardson, Thomas Say, and Israel Pemberton were appointed "to make a general state of the accounts of the Association, to be laid before the General meeting to-morrow."

19th Fourth Month. The above committee presented to the Trustees "an essay of the state of accounts."

"John Reynell's account for a piece of stroud, furnished at last treaty, at nine pounds ten shillings, and Joseph Richardson, silver-smith's account for ten pounds nineteen shillings, were examined, approved, and ordered to be paid."

The committee appointed to examine the Treasurer's account, report viz. :—

"We, the subscribers, pursuant to the appointment of the board of Trustees of the Friendly Association, &c., having examined the accounts of John Reynell, Treasurer, do find that he has received from sundry members of the said Association, the sum of one thousand three hundred and eight pounds eighteen shillings and one pence, and that he has paid by order of the said Trustees, the sum of eight hundred and eighty-eight pounds six pence half-penny, so that there remains in the hands of the said Treasurer, four hundred and twenty pounds eight shillings and six pence half-penny.

---

* It is not within the limits of a paper like this, to give a detailed statement of the rise and workings of a similar society in a neighboring State. Suffice it to say, that on the 16th of Fourth Month, 1757, the " New Jersey Association for helping the Indians " was organized. The members and contributions were as follows :—Daniel Smith £2c, Samuel Smith £20, John Smith £50, Joshua Raper £6, Joseph Noble £5 8s., William Heulings £5, Elizabeth Smith £16, Richard Smith £5, Thomas Wetherill £4, William Hartshorne £3, Jonathan Smith £3, John Hoskins £2, Hannah Hartshorne £4 9s, Daniel Smith, Jr. £5, Scamon Rodman £5, Samuel Rodman £5, Patience Clews £1, John Woolman £6, Edward Cathral £5 8s. Total, £171 5s. The above association was only in existence a very brief time.

this nineteenth day of the Fourth Month, 1757. We likewise find, there have been sundry orders drawn by the said Trustees on the said Treasurer, and not yet paid by him, amounting to four hundred and twenty-seven pounds nineteen shillings and ten pence.

" Witness our hands.

"ISRAEL PEMBERTON,
"THOMAS SAY,
"JOSEPH RICHARDSON."

"'The general state of the accounts of the Association, being prepared by the committee appointed to that service, was this day laid before the General Meeting of the members of the Association."

"At a *General* meeting of the members of the Friendly Association, &c., this nineteenth day of the Fourth Month, 1757, in the Schoolhouse." Present twenty-three Friends. A committee of nine, was appointed to examine the accounts of the Association as presented by the Trustees. Then adjourned until 2 o'clock in the afternoon.

P. M., near the time appointed, fifty-eight Friends met. The committee on accounts reported them correct, and further say, "there is in the hands of Jeremiah Warder, a parcel of goods remaining of the presents provided for the last treaty, belonging to this Association, amounting, as per list annexed, to about two hundred and forty pounds."

The minutes of the Trustees, since the last General Meeting, were read and approved.

" The Trustees observing that in the articles agreed on at the last General Meeting, their power of disposing of the stock of this Association is not so clearly expressed, but that some doubt may arise concerning the same ; therefore, it is now unanimously agreed that the Trustees should have power, not only to purchase goods for the Indians at treaties and for defraying the expenses of such Indian children as they may educate and take under their care, but likewise in any other manner, to advocate and promote the purpose of our Association, as they may apprehend circumstances may from time to time require."

An election was then held, which resulted in retaining the same Treasurer and all the former Trustees, except Benjamin Lightfoot; Peter Worrall, being substituted for him.

"A committee was chosen to take an obligation from each of the Trustees, in the sum of two hundred pounds (the amount now agreed upon), pursuant to the articles of the Association, &c., and the Trustees, obligees, and Treasurer, agreed to meet together on Fifth day next, at five o'clock in the afternoon, in the Schoolhouse, in order to execute the bonds, and proceed on business.

" The consideration of the value of the presents designed for the Indians, at the treaties to be held with them in a short time, is referred to the determination of the Trustees and Treasurer now chosen, as it cannot certainly be known what will be expedient to be done therein, until all the Indians who are expected, come in, and the time and place for the treaty be fixed.

" The *General* meeting then adjourned."

21st of Fourth Month. The Trustees, obligees, and Treasurer, met pursuant to adjournment. The latter issued an obligation to the former, in the penalty of two thousand pounds, for the faithful performance of his trust, &c., and all the Trustees executed a paper to the obligees chosen for similar reasons, agreeable to the rules of the Association.

It was unanimously agreed to meet on the Third day of the first week in every month, at three o'clock in the afternoon, or more frequently, if, in the opinion of the Clerk and three Trustees, it shall be deemed necessary. A committee was appointed to revise the minutes of former meetings, and to compare the originals with the copies entered in the book. Adjourned.

26th of Fourth Month. Abel James was chosen Clerk. It was agreed to meet at five o'clock on Third-day afternoon of each week, " till after the conclusion of the next Indian treaty, and that the Clerk shall give notice of all occasional meetings, at least four hours before the time fixed for meeting, to such of the Trustees who may not be present when such meetings are agreed on. And that every Trustee wholly absent from our meetings, shall pay a fine of two shillings, and for not attending in time, one shilling; the time to be determined by Thomas Stretch's standard clock. Jonathan Mifflin is desired to collect the fines. And it is likewise agreed, that any person leaving the company before the business is finished and the minutes are read, without the leave of the board, shall be fined one shilling."

An occasional meeting was held on the 2d of Fifth Month. "Joseph Morris, Thomas Say, Peter Worrall, Jeremiah Warder, and Richard Wistar, are desired to collect sundry goods now agreed on, and the list thereof delivered them, and hire a wagon to carry them to Lancaster."

Here several blank pages occur in the minute-book, to be filled, no doubt, with an account of the conference at Lancaster, which the Clerk omitted to transcribe.*

This treaty was not productive of much good. General Johnson had sent a delegation, numbering about one hundred and fifty, from the Six Nations. They met at Lancaster, on the 27th of Third Month, and there awaited the arrival of Teedyuscung and some Seneca Indians. But a month passed, and the expected Indians not arriving, Croghan sent messengers to Philadelphia, inviting the Governor to come up, and on the 9th of Fifth Month he reached Lancaster. It is not now

---

* I find, from some other minutes in my possession, that all the Trustees and the Treasurer attended the treaty at Lancaster, "except Abel James, who was debarred at home by the indisposition of his family."

known, what members of the Friendly Association accompanied him. On the 12th, he had a meeting with the Six Nations, when he asked their chief what he could do to promote peace with the Delawares, who had, until a recent date, been dependent upon the Six Nations, but now avowed that they would no longer have any but the Senecas, as their "Uncles and Superiors." The chief replied, that the Governor had better send to the Senecas and Delawares and ask them. Croghan insisted, however, that those assembled should state what they knew about the alleged frauds upon the Delawares or any other Indians, that he might apprise King George of the facts, and have matters adjusted, and urged upon them, if they failed herein, he (Croghan) would consider all such complaints, groundless.

The chief then stated, that the Delawares were aggrieved, first, because "one of their chiefs had been hanged in Jersey, for the accidental killing of a white man ; second, because a Shawnese warrior had died during imprisonment in Carolina; third, because both Shawnese and Delawares had been cheated out of their lands ; and fourth, because while the French settled among them, but received their provisions from over the water, the English settled and then *planted* among them, without remuneration, and as a matter of right."

They urged, however, a treaty with the Senecas and Delawares, as the most aggrieved parties. Accordingly, the Governor sent a messenger to Teedyuscung, informing him of what had passed at Lancaster, and requesting him to bring some Seneca chiefs to Easton at an early day, and promising that satisfaction would be rendered the Delawares, if it could be clearly proven, that they had been defrauded. In the Seventh Month following, Teedyuscung, accompanied by some Seneca and Six Nation chiefs, &c., in all about three hundred Indians, arrived at the place designated. What occurred on that occasion, will be described in its proper place.

The next meeting of the Trustees and Treasurer of the Friendly Association, took place on the 7th of Sixth Month, 1757. The Treasurer was authorized to receive subscriptions to the funds without interest, until the 5th of Eighth Month. A committee to collect and examine accounts was appointed, and the meeting adjourned.

5th of Seventh Month. Trustees again met. The account of Joseph Richardson, (silversmith) was presented and referred to the appropriate committee.

"Israel Pemberton produced a letter from Timothy Horsefield, at Bethlehem, dated yesterday, advising that the bearer was an express to the Governor, with letters from Colonel Weiser, stating that Teedyuscung was coming, who had sent a messenger to Fort Allen with a belt of wampum, to notify that he would be at the fort on the 5th inst., and at Easton on the 13th. Therefore Israel Pemberton, Jeremiah Warder, William Callender, William Fisher, and Joseph Morris are appointed a committee to confer with the Speaker of the House of Assembly and the Commissioners, respecting the approaching treaty, and likewise to make the necessary provision for a suitable present from this Association to Teedyuscung and the Indians who may come with him, and speak with them about sending up the Indians now in town, to meet Teedyuscung, particularly Philip, the Indian mentioned at the treaty last fall, as being then confined in the Jerseys from his wife and family.

"An abridgment of Samuel Hopkins' historical memoirs, relating to the Housantonick Indians, having been made by Charles Thomson, and lately read at a meeting of the board, the publication of which it is thought may be of service, therefore, Israel Pemberton,

William Callender, and Owen Jones, are desired to treat about printing it, and to engage to take such a number of copies, as they may find necessary to encourage the immediate publication of it.

"Israel Pemberton now acquaints us, that General Johnson has paid into the hands of Samuel Burling, the sum of one hundred and fifty pounds lent George Croghan before the Lancaster treaty, and that said Samuel Burling, has, by order of Israel Pemberton, purchased some goods suitable for Indians, not to be procured here, amounting to more than one hundred and fifty pounds; therefore the appropriate committee is desired to inspect the account thereof, that the Treasurer may pay the balance."

9th of Seventh Month. The committee on accounts, reported that Joseph Richardson's bill for silver medals, &c., amounted to one hundred and thirty-two pounds eleven shillings and six pence, which the meeting ordered the Treasurer to pay.

"11th of Seventh Month. The committee appointed to wait upon the Speaker of the House of Assembly and the Commissioners, report, that this day they waited upon the latter (the Speaker not being in town), and being informed that the Governor intended to set off very soon for Easton, to attend the treaty, they had likewise waited upon the Governor, to know when the treaty was likely to begin more certainly, and to desire the continuance of his approbation of our attendance as heretofore, with such a present to the Indians as we might offer, to be delivered by him in our behalf, upon which he gave the committee the following answer in writing :—

"GENTLEMEN :—The Proprietaries have acquainted me, that the Earl of Halifax has communicated to them, with very strong expressions of dissatisfaction, a treaty held with the Indians at Philadelphia, by the people called Quakers, which his Lordship was pleased to think the most extraordinary procedure, he had ever seen in persons who are on the same footing only, with all others of the King's private subjects, to presume to treat with *Foreign Princes;* and further, that as the suffering any one part of the King's subjects, whether of a different profession of religion, or however else distinguished, to treat, or act as mediators between a Province in which they live, and any independent people, is the highest invasion of his Majesty's Prerogative Royal, and of the worst consequence, as it must tend to divide the King's subjects into different parties and interests ; and by how much more these or any other body of people are suffered to attach the Indians to their own particular interest, by so much less, must their regard to people of other professions be. The Proprietaries, therefore, have directed me not to suffer these people or any other body or particular Society in Pennsylvania, to concern themselves in any treaty with the Indians, or on any pretense to suffer presents from such persons to be given to the Indians, or to be joined with the public present at any such treaty. These directions I shall conform to, and my regard for you, as well as Mr. Penn's instructions, leads me to observe, it would be prudent in you to decline going in a body, your attendance at treaties as a distinct Society, having given great offence to the ministry.

"July 11th, 1757.　　　　　　　"WILLIAM DENNY."

The committee then assured the Governor, that the charges contained in this letter, must have arisen from misrepresentations of the conduct of Friends, and an impartial inquiry, would satisfy him that they were unjust.

The meeting requested the committee, to prepare a "memorial or address" to be presented to the Governor, giving a true account of the design of the Association, and of the conduct of its members at treaties, to be brought to the next meeting. Adjourned.

On the 13th of Seventh Month, the committee produced their address, which was deliberated upon, and, with some amendments, unanimously agreed to by the members present. The clerk was authorized to sign it on behalf of the board, and to accompany those who prepared it, and to present it to the Governor.

The address, which is a long and able document, is published in "Hazard's Register," vol. v., page 363. It sets forth, by way of preface, the melancholy condition of the Province, owing largely to the alienation of hitherto friendly Indians, and of the desire Friends had, as loyal, peace-loving subjects, to assist in the restoration of friendship and peace. The Governor is reminded, that Friends at first took no very active part in these matters, which belonged to those concerned in the administration of the government, but, nevertheless, printed in the "Gazette," some reasons which contributed to this unhappy rupture, that public attention might be directed thereto ; and, moreover, they urged upon the Assembly repeatedly, to "use every rational method" to ascertain why, and wherein the Indians were aggrieved ; but say they, the Assembly, declined this advice, and made appropriations for the erection of forts on the frontiers, and for military purposes, in the hope thereby to defend the settlers, but in fact to increase the general desolation and distress ; and when Governor Morris declared war, Friends urged him to reconsider it, and offered to surrender "a much larger part of their estates than the heaviest taxes of a war could be expected to require," if thereby the peaceful purposes of the Association, might be carried out. They then reiterate the history of their labors at treaties, and lay before the Governor, in general terms, much of what has been previously narrated in detail, dwelling particularly upon the fact that hostilities ceased temporarily, when the Indians were informed that there was a willingness on the part of the government, to hear and remedy their grievances ; and that Teedyuscung declined to enter upon business, unless the Quakers were permitted to be present at the Easton treaty.

Friends tell Governor Denny, that he declared to them his approval of their conduct, and solicited their co-operation, and they now are at a loss to know wherein they have forfeited his esteem, unless their application to the Secretary for an inspection of the records in his office, produced that effect. "If," say they, "that should be the case, and the intention and manner of that application has been misrepresented by any of the Proprietaries' agents, and others engaged with them, in the measures which have contributed to the present unhappy circumstances of this Province, we think it necessary to inform the Governor, that this Province was settled on terms very different from most of the other colonies. The first adventurers were men of substance and reputation, who purchased the lands of the Proprietor ; and as he obliged himself and his heirs, by an express covenant, contained in their original deeds, ' to clear the land from all titles, claims, and demands of the Indian natives, or any other persons whatsoever,' they agreed to pay an annual quit-rent, more than sufficient to enable him to satisfy the Indians. and obtain a peaceable possession of the land ; and during the lives of our first Proprietor, and the first settlers, we believe this was faithfully performed ; and so large a balance remained towards making further purchases, as the settlement of the country increased, that any attempt to elude the original intention and agreement, of fairly purchasing the land of the people who had a native right in it, will be ever condemned by all impartial and honest men."

Friends further declare, that as the Indians complained of frauds, and requested that members of the Association should impartially examine into the matter, they felt themselves under the most solemn obligation to comply with so reasonable a demand, and presumed that the Governor and Secretary would aid them in so doing. They desired that all people, of every religious denomination, would join with them in the good work of promoting peace, and hoped, that the Governor was convinced of their integrity, and was willing to disabuse the minds of others, of any false impressions concerning them. They conclude this interesting paper as follows :—

"We apprehend our duty to God, and the King, have engaged us in this business : and some of the good effects thereof, have already appeared. We, therefore, now again offer the Governor, to contribute something considerable towards the present necessary to be made to the Indians, at the ensuing treaty, and by our personal attendance, to improve the confidence and good opinion these people have of us, to the public benefit. Should the Governor persist in refusing to accept our present, we assure him we shall not, by our conduct, give any just occasion to charge us with disrespect towards him ; and we desire our attendance at the treaty, may not be considered as such. The business to be transacted there is of so much consequence, to the lives, liberties, and properties, of the people of this Province. that should we omit to attend there, and depend upon the Governor and the King's agent receiving all the information on this important occasion from the Proprietaries' agents and others, who have for some years past been concerned in transacting Indian affairs, we should be deficient in our duty as Christians and Englishmen,—denominations we hold more dear to us than any other titles or appellations, whatsoever.

"(Signed)   "ABEL JAMES,
"Clerk.
"PHILADELPHIA, 14th Seventh Month, 1757."

Israel Pemberton, William Callender, and William Fisher, (the committee who prepared the above essay), reported to the meeting, held on the 14th of Seventh Month, that they delivered the address to the Governor, as requested, who promised to read and deliberately consider it, and assured them, that although their views, if carried out, would be serviceable, yet he was determined not to depart from the instructions he had received from England, and peremptorily refused to reason with them upon the subject.

The committee on goods, stated that they had added to the stock on hand, in the hope that all objections against their making presents, would be removed at this time, as on a former occasion. The meeting ordered, that an assortment of goods be packed ready for shipment, to an amount not exceeding five hundred pounds, to be sent to Easton, when ordered by such of the Trustees, as expected to attend the proposed treaty.

The committee on the address, were directed to re-visit the Governor, and ask his consent to print his written answer with the address, in order to remove "the prejudices and false reports" which had been detrimental to the Association. Should he permit the publication of his answer, these Friends were authorized to have the printing done at once; if not, they were to get the address published by itself. Adjourned.

15th of Seventh Month. The committee apprised the meeting, that they had called upon the Governor, but he being in Council, could not be interviewed. His Secretary promised to acquaint him with their wishes, which being done, the Governor replied in writing, as follows:—

"PHILADELPHIA, 15th July, 1757, 12 o'clock.

"GENTLEMEN:—As you know I am desired and most strictly enjoined, not to suffer any particular body or society to concern themselves in treaties with Indians, or on any pretense to give presents to them, it is out of my power to permit your presents to be given. I shall once more repeat my advice:—You would do well, to decline appearing at the ensuing treaty in a body, your attendance at treaties as a distinct society, having given great offense to the Ministry.

"WILLIAM DENNY.

"To Mr. ISRAEL PEMBERTON, and the other gentlemen."

On the same day, at 2 o'clock, another communication was received from the Governor, as follows :—

"GENTLEMEN :—Your address, in some parts of it which relate to transactions that have passed since my administration, misrepresents several important facts, and contains some reflections on the conduct of the Proprietaries and their agents here, in managing the affairs of the Indians, which I hope will be found to be without the least foundation. I cannot therefore conceive it seasonable or proper at this time, for you to print it, especially when it is considered that the publishing it, may tend to inflame the minds of the Indians, and obstruct the business of the ensuing treaty at Easton, where the complaints made by them, will be fully and impartially heard, and I hope fully accommodated.
"WILLIAM DENNY.

"To ISRAEL PEMBERTON, and the other gentlemen."

After careful consideration of the above letters, the meeting agreed to return an answer thereto in writing, which was as follows :—

"May it please the Governor :
"Nothing less than a regard to the public interest, would engage us to decline fully complying with the Governor's advice not to attend the ensuing Indian treaty, though we have reason to believe that the Proprietaries' instructions to the Governor on this occasion, are grounded on some false and unjust information sent from hence.
"Our application this day was to desire, the Governor would be so kind as to inform us whether he had any objections to our printing his answer, in which the Earl of Halifax is said to have called the Indians 'foreign princes and an independent people,' but the answer the Governor has now been pleased to send us, relates solely to our address. As it is contrary to our intention to misrepresent any transaction before or since the Governor's administration, we shall esteem it a favor, to have those parts pointed out which the Governor thinks in any respect exceptionable.
"What we have said concerning the Proprietaries and their agents, is grounded on the public records.

"The Governor's refusing to accept of our contribution, or our offer of attending the treaty, has given much encouragement to the adversaries of the peace of the Province, to repeat their malevolent aspersions and calumnies against us; but to manifest our regard to the public interest to be greater than to our private characters, we shall for a few days suspend the printing of our address, that there may be no possibility of charging us, by its publication, 'with inflaming the minds of the Indians.'

"Signed by appointment, and on behalf of the Trustees and Treasurer of the Friendly Association for Regaining and Preserving Peace with the Indians by Pacific Measures, this 15th of Seventh Month, 1757.

"ABEL JAMES,

"*Clerk.*"

The next meeting of the Association (which was an unimportant one) was held on the 5th of Ninth Month, and during the interim, the treaty at Easton had taken place. Several blank pages are left in the "minute-book" wherein to record what transpired on that occasion, which, however, has been neglected. It would be interesting to know what effect the above letter had upon Governor Denny, but the book is silent upon the subject. That members of the Association attended the treaty is evident, and that some of the goods obtained for presents to the Indians, were sold to the Commissioners by the Friends, during the treaty, will appear subsequently.

From Charles Thomson's notes on that occasion, we are informed that Teedyuscung, accompanied by delegations from the Six Nations and Seneca Tribes, (in all some three hundred Indians), arrived at Easton about the middle of the Seventh Month. Here they were met by Governor Denny, six of his Council, four Commissioners, the Speaker of the House of Assembly, and a number of citizens. Before proceedings commenced, Teedyuscung insisted that Charles Thomson should be his clerk, which, after an altercation lasting four days, was acceded to. This request was made because on a former occasion, when complaints were urged against the Proprietaries, the Secretary of the Province declined to record them. The Governor opened the conference by informing Teedyuscung, that he had laid the proceedings of the former treaty before Sir William Johnson, who had deputed George Croghan, his Secretary and agent, to attend on that occasion, and inquire into every grievance they had suffered; whereupon Croghan solemnly assured them in a brief speech that "he would do everything in his power to have all differences amicably adjusted to their satisfaction, agreeable to his orders and instructions." Teedyuscung, in responding, reiterated the statements made at the last treaty, and referred the Governor and his people "to their own hearts and writings for the truth of what he said." The burden of his speech, was, that the Indians had been deceived and cheated of their lands, and that he demanded justice—nothing more— which, if obtained, would secure a lasting peace. He insisted, moreover, that the boundaries be fixed between the Indians and the whites, and expressed the wishes of his people, to be instructed in the Christian religion and the arts of civilized life, by such persons as should be agreeable to them.

Teedyuscung had been freely supplied with "fire-water," and was intoxicated when he made this speech; so the next morning, when sober, Croghan challenged him to repeat it, thereby intending, evidently, to confuse him; but he accepted the challenge, and with much plainness and minuteness of detail, went over the whole ground, and, in conclusion, demanded payment for lands taken from his people by fraud.

Notwithstanding the expressed willingness of the Governor and Croghan at the beginning of the conference, to redress the wrongs of the natives, the former, after the delivery of Teedyuscung's speech, referred him to Sir William Johnson; but as his agent was present, with power to act, the Chief declined the proposal.

Teedyuscung asserted, as another reason for his refusal, that he had never met with Johnson, and that delay might result in war. He did not demand immediate payment, but would wait until the King was heard from, before whom he requested their grievances should be laid as soon as possible. He expressly insisted, that certain deeds (or copies of them) be produced and transmitted to England, containing evidence that the Indians had been defrauded of lands. If this were done, he offered to confirm a peace at once. The Governor expressed himself as willing to grant this reasonable request, but privately agreed with Weiser and Croghan, not to present the papers most desired by the Chief.

Two days thereafter, during which time the Indians had been kept under the influence of alcoholic liquors, Denny presented to Teedyuscung, several deeds as the ones asked for, and desired that all further debate between them should cease, until time was had to send them to England, and await the answer of the King. This proposition was accepted by the Chief in good faith, without any examination of the documents; and thereupon Teedyuscung, in the name of his people, solemnly concluded a peace.

Subsequent investigation, disclosed the fact that the deeds produced were not those demanded; but no public notice of this fact was taken for fear of dissatisfying the Indians, and because it was hoped that the Governor, would, upon deliberation, order what papers were necessary, to be forwarded to the King.

Charles Thomson, in concluding his narrative of the Easton treaty, says:—

"Here, then, the affair rests. If the proper papers, and a true state of the case be laid before the King and Council for a just determination; if the Indians be secured in their property, and instructed in religion and the civil arts, agreeable to their request, and the trade with them, regulated, and set on such a footing that they may be secure from abuse, there is not the least doubt but the alliance and friendship of the Indians may be forever secured to the British interest; but should these things be neglected, the arms of the French are open to receive them. Whether for the future they are to be our friends, or enemies, seems now to be in our own power. Whether another such opportunity will ever return, is altogether uncertain. It becomes men of wisdom and prudence, to leave nothing to chance, where reason can decide."

Thus ended a glaringly disgraceful meeting. When the trickery there practiced, was discovered by the unsuspecting Indians, fuel was added to the flame of their indignation.

The next meeting of the Trustees, was held on the 4th of Tenth Month, 1757, at the house of Alexander Seaton. Present, sixteen members. Sundry accounts, amounting in the aggregate to two hundred and eighty-nine pounds fourteen shillings ten pence, were presented, and orders drawn on the Treasurer for the same. It was, however, declared, that—

"As there are demands now against us, amounting to a larger sum of money than we have in hand, the Treasurer is desired to request Isaac Norris, Speaker of the late Assembly, to repay the one hundred pounds lent the Assembly last winter.

"The Trustees who attended the last treaty at Easton, having while there, agreed to sell the Provincial Commissioners ten pieces of

strouds, at *eleven* pounds per piece, and two and a half pieces of
blankets, at ten pounds per piece, and some other smaller articles,
Jeremiah Warder is desired to receive the money for the same, and
pay it to the Treasurer; and he is likewise to account for four pieces of
stript duffells, sold by him last winter to the Provincial Commissioners.

"It being notified, that a son of Seneca George, an Indian of
note, has been some time in the city, having had the small-pox, and
is now in want of clothing, Isaac Zane and Jeremiah Warder, are
desired to give him such things as are immediately necessary, and
to send him to school, if he can be persuaded duly to attend
there.

"Israel Pemberton, William Callender, Peter Worrall, Thomas
Say, and the Clerk, are desired to write to John Jones and Thomas
Evans, of Gwynned; to Samuel Foulke, of Richland; to Thomas
Carleton and William Harvey, of Kennett; George Ashbridge and
Aaron Ashbridge, of Goshen; Francis Parvin and Benjamin Lightfoot, of Maiden Creek, to engage these Friends to collect the money
subscribed by contributors in their respective neighborhoods, as it
is now much wanted. Abraham Dawes, from Plymouth, and George
Miller, from Providence, being now present, are desired to undertake
the same in their several and respective neighborhoods, and the
above-named Trustees, are desired to write to John Morris, requesting him to assist Abraham Dawes therein." Adjourned.

At a meeting on the 11th of Tenth Month, accounts
were presented and examined, being principally for
advances made to the Association by individual members, amounting in the aggregate, to five hundred and
thirty pounds four shillings and five pence. An order
was drawn on the Treasurer, signed by all present, and
that officer was authorized to receive, one hundred and
fifty pounds, from Israel Pemberton, and one hundred and seventy-five pounds six shillings and eight
pence from Jeremiah Warder.

The committee on accounts made report, that there
were at Easton, in the hands of Jost Vollert, six
pieces of stroud, four pieces of match coats, and one
piece of flowered serge, the value being about one

hundred and five pounds; that Jeremiah Warder had two bales and ten pieces of striped blankets; that Israel Pemberton, had six silver medals and chains, thirty-three medals without chains, four silver ornaments, six shells, and two belts of wampum, returned from the Ohio Indians; at Isaac Zane's house there were fifteen silver medals and dial compasses, and at Joseph Richardson's, a pair of stamps for medals; all the property of the Association. Then adjourned.

On the 1st of Eleventh Month, another meeting was held, at which it was made known that there was due Samuel Neave, for three pieces of strouds, not previously noted, the sum of thirty pounds, for which amount an order was drawn on the Treasurer.

"Joseph Morris and the Clerk, are added to the committee appointed to revise the minutes of the Association to be sent to our Friends in England." Adjourned.

On the 3d of Twelfth Month, this committee reported progress, and the meeting adjourned to re-assemble to-morrow afternoon, at 2 o'clock, "at William Callender's, to read over the fair copy which was now produced."

On the next day, eleven Friends met at time and place appointed.

"The minutes from the beginning, to the General meeting on the 19th of Fourth Month, 1757, were read, and it is agreed, when the transcribing is completed, they be delivered to our esteemed friend John Hunt, to be made such use of, as himself and other judicious Friends in London, may agree shall be necessary."

On the 6th of Twelfth Month, there were present at Alexander Seaton's, thirteen Friends. The following appears on the minutes, under that date :—

"Being reminded that the proceedings of this Government in building houses for the Indians, at Wyoming, agreeable to the promises made them at the late treaty at Easton, was delayed until the season of the year was so far advanced, that, from the accounts we have from the Commissioners concerned therein, as well as from Teedyuscung, it was not convenient to proceed so far therein as to encourage the Indians to settle there this fall and winter. And as we are fully convinced that an early application to complete that business next spring, may contribute much to their settling, and re-establish peace with the Indians, and as Teedyuscung expressly told us, a few days since, in this city, that their dependence was upon Friends, to have the same put forward so early next spring that the houses may be finished time enough to accommodate and encourage the Indians to come and settle there before the season for planting their corn, &c. commences, therefore, Israel Pemberton, Joseph Morris, Jeremiah Warder, and Jonathan Mifflin, are desired to converse with the Speaker of the House of Assembly and the Commissioners on that subject, and acquaint them with our desire and readiness to do anything therein in our power, to answer the expectations of the Indians, and promote the good work of peace. And if upon such a conference, it appears to the committee that we can be serviceable therein, they report the same to our next meeting."

13th of Twelfth Month. The committee reported progress, and were continued.

At the meetings on the 20th and 27th of Twelfth Month, no business of importance was transacted, nor is mention made of the above committee making further report until the 24th of the Third Month following, which will appear in proper place. Thus ended this year's business. During 1757, Friends throughout the city and country, had contributed to the treasury of the Association, but there is no data by which to approximate even to the amount subscribed.

On the 3d of First Month, 1758, fourteen Friends convened at the usual place, and after some general conversation, adjourned until the 10th, at which meeting nothing of interest transpired, and Friends adjourned until the 17th.

A minute of the 17th reads as follows:—

"It being remarked, that by account lately received of the situation of the Indians settled at Pennsbury, it appears likely they may be in want of a supply of provisions for their present relief, for more perfect intelligence of their circumstance, and that we may have it in our power to administer to their necessities if there should be occasion, Jeremiah Warder and Isaac Zane, offer to take a journey to visit them, which being well approved of, it is agreed that they have liberty to lay out a sum of money, not exceeding ten pounds, in corn or other provisions, if they find it necessary, to be distributed amongst them in such manner as they may deem most conducive to their help and assistance, which we shall take care to repay."

No further business appearing, adjourned to meet at the usual time and place.

On the 24th of First Month, a committee of four Friends was appointed to examine the list of contributors to this Association, ascertain who have not paid their subscriptions, "and write to such Friends as may be most likely to assist them in collecting the same. Such as do not pay upon application to them, are to be requested to sign obligations for their several subscriptions." Adjourned.

At the next meeting, on the 31st, the above committee reported progress and were continued, as also on the 7th of Second Month.

Nothing further of interest occurs, until the meeting

on the 14th of Third Month, when five lists of delinquent
city subscribers were furnished by a committee. These
were given to sundry members to collect, "as soon
as may be." And it was unanimously agreed, that the
sums originally subscribed may be received without
accrued interest, until the meeting shall otherwise direct. "The Treasurer is desired to furnish the Trustees
with a sufficient number of blank receipts, signed by
him, to be filled up and given to those who pay, and
that such subscribers as do not pay, be asked to give
their notes, payable with interest from the date of the
subscription papers, and the Treasurer is desired to
furnish blank notes to answer that occasion." Then
adjourned until the 24th of Third Month.

Under the last-mentioned date appears the following interesting minute:—

"Upon consideration of the just expectations which the Indians
(with whom this Province has held treaties for peace at Easton and
Lancaster) have, that the engagements of this Government be complied with, as the Governor promised they should be, and especially
when, by a message received by this Government, it appears there
is a favorable prospect of extending and confirming the peace so
much desired to several other nations, to the great advantage of
the British interest; and, as the Trustees and Treasurer are informed that the treasury of the Province is exhausted, and they
continuing desirous to do all in their power to promote peace, in a
manner consistent with our profession, do unanimously agree to
offer the Assembly of this Province, such sums of money as they
may want, to enable the Governor to fulfill his said engagements; to
be paid to the Commissioners or such persons as they may appoint,
and to be repaid, out of the Provincial Treasury, when it can be
conveniently done. And Israel Pemberton, James Pemberton,
Jeremiah Warder, Richard Wistar, Owen Jones, and Abel James,
are appointed, to prepare an essay of an address to the Assembly,
representing the same, to be brought here to-morrow morning at
nine o'clock, to which time we adjourn."

The above committee were present with the address the next morning, which was approved, ordered to be copied and signed by the clerk, "and he, with William Callender, Joseph Richardson, Richard Wistar, and William Fisher, are to deliver the same to the House of Representatives this morning." The address is as follows:—

"To the Representatives of the Freemen of the Province of Pennsylvania, in General Assembly met:—The address of the Trustees and Treasurer of the Friendly Association for Regaining and Preserving Peace with the Indians by Pacific Measures, respectfully showeth, that as we have, with the approbation of the Government, at several treaties held with the Indians at Easton and Lancaster, contributed freely towards the presents made to the Indians, and defraying the expenses of the messengers sent by the King's Deputy agent, to invite the Indians on the Ohio to renew their alliance with the Crown of Great Britain;—and as, by the blessing of Divine Providence, pacific measures have so far succeeded, that from the message now received from eight tribes of those western and other distant Indians, it appears there are just grounds to hope for the establishment of peace with them, and the engaging a considerable number with whom this Government has not been acquainted, to enter into the alliance, we are heartily disposed to promote so desirable a service, and thereby to give a renewed testimony of our loyalty to our Gracious King, and our sincere concern to advance the cause and interest of the Christian religion, and the peace and prosperity of our country. And being informed that the public treasury is exhausted, lest these salutary measures should thereby be delayed, and the promises made by the Governor, in behalf of this Province, remain unperformed, we think it our duty, to acquaint you, that out of the fund of our Association we are willing to supply you with such sums of money as may be immediately necessary for carrying on these negotiations towards re-establishing peace with the Indians, and to wait for the repayment of the money, out of the Public Treasury, till it can be conveniently done. If our proposal appears to you, to be conducive to the public advantage, and meets with your approbation, we shall immediately direct our Treasurer to pay the Provincial

Commissioners, or such other committee as you may be pleased to appoint, such sum or sums, as on consideration, you may judge these exigencies may require. Signed by order and on behalf of said Trustees and Treasurer.

"ABEL JAMES,
"*Clerk.*"

At the meeting on the 4th of Fourth Month, the committee reported, they had attended to their appointment, and had received from Joseph Fox, a member of the house, a copy of the resolutions that body passed after reading the address, as follows:—

"*Resolved,* That the thanks of this House be given to the said Society, for their friendly and generous offer.

"*Resolved,* That this House do recommend it to the Provincial Commissioners, to borrow of said Friendly Society, such sum or sums of money as may be sufficient to answer the present Indian demands; and that the Representatives will use their care and endeavors to secure the repayment thereof, when further supplies shall be raised for the public service."

It was now unanimously agreed, that an order be drawn, on John Reynell, treasurer, in favor of Joseph Fox, for one hundred pounds, which was accordingly done, and was signed by eleven Trustees. A committee of four was appointed to prepare a statement of accounts of the Association from the last General Meeting, to be laid before the next General Meeting on the 19th. A list of subscribers was made out, and certain Friends were authorized to apprise them of the time of the General Meeting, as then, an election was to be held for Trustees and Treasurer, to serve one year, for whom they are entitled to vote. Adjourned.

At a meeting of the Association, held on the 11th of Fourth Month, Thomas Wharton, executor to the estate

of Thomas Davis, deceased, presented through the
Clerk, a bill for needles and fish-hooks, furnished by
Thomas Davis to the Trustees at the last treaties held
at Lancaster and Easton, amounting to two pounds
ten shillings, which was ordered paid.

" Teedyuscung and some other Indians being come to town, and
it appearing to us that this Government, complying with its engagements in completing the houses at Wyoming as soon as possible, to
encourage the Indians to plant and settle there this spring, is a
matter of great importance to the people of the Province, therefore, Israel Pemberton, James Pemberton, Owen Jones, Abel James,
and Joseph Morris, are appointed a committee to converse with the
members of the Governor's Council, (the Governor being absent
at this time in the three lower counties) and the Provincial Commissioners, and to acquaint them, that agreeable to our offer to the
House of Assembly of the 25th ultimo, this Association continues
willing to furnish money as then proposed, to enable them immediately to prosecute the erecting and completing the said buildings,
and such other purposes as money may be wanted for, to promote
and establish peace with the Indians." Adjourned.

Space is here left in the book, with the obvious
intent of recording the minutes of the General Meeting
which occurred on the 19th. In the absence of any
such minutes, it is presumable that a synopsis of the
year's business was laid before the Friends assembled
at this meeting, as on a former occasion. Most of the
Trustees, the Treasurer, and Clerk were re-elected to
serve another year, as appears from the proceedings of
a subsequent meeting. Edward Pennington, Jacob
Lewis, and Jacob Shoemaker, Jr., were chosen Trustees,
in place of Abram Dawes, Jonathan Mifflin, and George
Miller, which is the only change noted. At the meeting on the 27th of Fourth Month, John Reynell, Treasurer, executed a bond, in the sum of two thousand
pounds, to the Trustees, for the faithful performance of

88

his trust, John Pemberton being his surety as heretofore. The Trustees, likewise executed an obligation to sixteen members of the Association, in the city and elsewhere, in a similar sum, to fulfil the duties required of them.

On the 2d of Fifth Month, it was unanimously concluded to meet hereafter, on the Fifth day of the first week in every month, at 5 o'clock in the afternoon, at the house of Alexander Seaton, or more frequently, "if in the opinion of four Trustees it shall be deemed necessary." It was further agreed, that "Israel Pemberton, Isaac Zane, Jacob Shoemaker, Jeremiah Warder, and the Clerk, shall be a committee, to perform such lesser services as may occur, and not require the calling all the Trustees together. The Clerk was authorized to give four hours' notice of all occasional meetings, to such Trustees as were not present when the time for such meetings was agreed upon, and that all the Trustees thus notified, if absent, shall pay a fine of two shillings; if late, one shilling; the time to be determined by Thomas Stretch's standard clock. Thomas Say to collect said fines." These rules did not apply to such Trustees as were Commissioners for the Indian trade, who were entirely exempt from all fines. Adjourned.

On the 20th of Fifth Month, an occasional meeting was held. The following is taken from the minutes:—

"The Governor of this Province, having lately given a commission to John Hughes and others, to hire workmen and go up to Wyoming, there to assist the Indians in building a town and making a settlement and opening a road to it, in pursuance of which, two of the said Commissioners (John Hughes and Henry Pauling) set out a few days since with a number of workmen; and we being now informed that Teedyuscung, the Delaware Chief, with his wife and family, and a considerable number of other Indians, joined them at Bethlehem, and went forward from thence on Third day (the 16th instant), so that there is a prospect of this necessary work being at last performed,—on consideration of which, the same motives which have heretofore induced us to engage in the desirable work of restoring peace still prevailing, and Isaac Zane, (of whose hearty and constant endeavors therein we have had abundant experience) now acquainting us that John Hughes had, before his setting out, signified to him that he was desirous of his company and assistance, which Isaac's state of health would not permit him then to offer; but he being now somewhat recovered and willing to go up to Wyoming, and assist the Provincial Commissioners in erecting the buildings and making the settlement proposed, it is unanimously agreed, that out of the fund of our Association, he shall be paid to his satisfaction for such service, and that he may take with him some carpenters, a mason, an interpreter, and such other assistance as he may think necessary. On his arrival at Wyoming, he is desired to offer his service to assist the Provincial Commissioners in the work, and if it should appear to him that anything more is necessary, than they are willing to get done at the public expense, either in building the houses, opening the road, or otherwise—in that case he is authorized to engage workmen, and get all such necessary matters accomplished, for all which it is agreed, he shall be paid out of the stock under our care. And for his present supply, an order is now drawn on the Treasurer, payable to him, for one hundred pounds, and signed by all the Trustees present but himself. Jeremiah Warder, Jacob Shoemaker, Israel and James Pemberton, are desired to assist him in procuring horses, and whatever else may be necessary, towards fitting him and his company for the journey." Adjourned.

"21st of Sixth Month, 1758. Being informed that the Commissioners for Indian affairs have recommended Nathaniel Holland as a suitable person for an agent at Fort Augusta (Sunbury), for negotiating and managing the trade with the Indians, agreeable to an Act of the General Assembly of this Province, and that the Governor has commissioned him, and the said act requiring that he should give security for his faithful performance of said trust, therefore the Trustees and Treasurer, consistent with their views of promoting the peace of this Province, and the good opinion they have of the said Holland, do request Israel Pemberton and Abel James, to join said Nathaniel Holland, in the bond which he is to execute, as his sureties, and do engage to stand jointly and equally bound with him, in behalf of this Association.

" The consideration of the circumstances of our country-folk now in captivity amongst the Indians, having been the frequent subject of our conversation, and now revived, it is agreed to desire the Commissioners for Indian affairs who are members of this Association, to confer with their brethren about it, and if they can concert any measures to answer that end, our stock for any sum not exceeding five hundred pounds, may be depended on to defray the expenses thereof, if wanted.

" The Treasurer informs the Trustees, that Joseph Fox, one of the Provincial Commissioners, has paid him the hundred pounds lent the Province some time since.

" Israel Pemberton and the other Friends of the Standing Committee, are desired to collect some suitable clothing and other necessaries for such of the thirteen Cherokees and other Indians now in this town, as they may see fit, and present them in behalf of the Friendly Association, as we apprehend it may have a tendency to promote the good work of peace." Then adjourned.

" On the 6th of Seventh Month, the Clerk notified the meeting, that Israel Pemberton declined to act as surety for Nathaniel Holland; whereupon, Joshua Howell offering to do it, he and Abel James, joined Nathaniel Holland, and executed the bond in the penalty of one thousand pounds, which was approved by the Trustees and Treasurer, who agree to be jointly and equally bound with them.

" The committee appointed at last meeting, report that they have furnished the Indians in town with some clothing and other necessaries, the cost of which they will state at a subsequent meeting.

" In consideration of Nathaniel Holland's having left his former employment, going up to Shamokin to act as clerk for John Carson, (late agent there for negotiating trade with the Indians) for less wages than he had at his former employment, (from a desire of being useful to the public), it is now agreed, that the Treasurer do pay to Israel Pemberton, in his behalf, out of the fund of this Association, fifteen pounds twelve shillings and six pence.

" 12th of Seventh Month. The Standing Committee are desired to distribute more clothing, and some silver medals, &c., to the Indians in town, to an amount not exceeding thirty pounds. No further business."

" 3d of Eighth Month. Jeremiah Warder, and James Drinker,

brought in their accounts against the Association, and a committee of three was appointed, to examine the same, and report at an early day ; also, to find out what is due by the Association.

" It was agreed, that the Standing Committee might, at their discretion, present the messengers now in town from the Seneca and Munsey Indians, with clothing, &c., to an amount not exceeding twenty pounds.   Adjourned."

" 7th of Ninth Month.   The committee on accounts, reported progress and were continued.   Information was given that a large number of Indians, from various tribes, were collecting at Easton, Wyoming, and Fort Allen (Weissport), preparatory to holding a treaty with the English Governor at the former place.   The meeting considered the question, what was the duty of the Association in the matter, but did not reach a conclusion.   Five Friends were appointed ' to confer with such members of the Governor's Council, and of the Provincial Assembly, as they can, and renew our assurances of our disposition to contribute our endeavors, to the completing of the work of peace, and extending the British interest with the Indians,' after which adjourned."

"At a meeting held on the 12th of Ninth Month, the committee on accounts, reported that there was due by the Association to sundry individuals, all members of the Association, sums amounting in the aggregate, to three hundred and thirty-six pounds nine shillings seven and a half pence.   On examining Isaac Zane's account of expenses to and at Wyoming, it was ascertained that of the one hundred pounds furnished him by the Treasurer, there was due from him to the Association, three pounds sixteen shillings and two pence.   Of goods, &c., belonging to the Association, William Fisher had 'three pieces of embossed serge, and four pieces half-thicks.'   Israel Pemberton, had ' four pieces striped blankets, part of a piece of yellow tamy, about forty thousand black and white wampum, twenty medals, three silver gorgets, and a gray mare.' Jost Vollert, residing at Easton, had 'six pieces stroud, four pieces match coats, and one piece of flowered serge.'   Jeremiah Warder, had 'ten pieces blankets,' and Isaac Zane, held 'fifteen medals, seventeen pocket-compasses, and three magnets.'

"After orders were drawn on the Treasurer, and signed by the Trustees for sums due, as above indicated, the meeting adjourned."

" 15th Ninth Month.   No quorum present."

I find among my papers, some copies of letters of above date, signed by that active member of this useful society, Israel Pemberton, addressed to influential Friends in different sections of the country, soliciting pecuniary aid and co-operation, to further the aims of the Association. No mention of his appointment to this service appearing upon the minutes, it is presumable that the interest he felt in the success of the work designed to be accomplished, led him to urge Friends to aid therein.*

On the 2d of Tenth Month, twelve members assembled. "Israel Pemberton produced a letter from our friends John Hunt, Richard How, John Fothergill, Thomas Corbyn, Jacob Hagen, Jr., and Robert Foster, dated London, 26th Fifth Month, 1758, advising that they had ordered a quantity of goods suitable for the Indians to be bought and shipped on board the 'Betsy Sally,' Edward Snead, master, which amounts with charges, to eight hundred and fifteen pounds two shillings and three pence; with a design to promote a commerce with the Indians at such places as would be acceptable to them; which letter, appears to have been wrote before they received an account of the late Act of Assembly of this Province for regulating the Indian trade; and as it appears to have been done from an anxious concern for the promotion of the welfare of this Province in particular, and the British colonies in America in general, without any advantage to themselves, it merits our grateful acknowledgment."

---

* " PHILADELPHIA, 15th Ninth Month, 1758.

" RESPECTED FRIEND :—As we expect in a short time, a large number of Indians to a Treaty with this Government at Easton, the Trustees of the Friendly Association, are apprehensive there may be occasion or more money than we have in stock, and therefore desire thee to apply to such Friends as belong to your Meeting and have not yet paid their subscriptions, and request them to pay the same to thee, or if there are any whom it will not suit immediately to pay, to get their notes for the sums they have subscribed.

" We are in hopes there may also be some among you, who on application, may be induced to subscribe towards this good work, to whom the service of it might not at first so fully appear. Thy endeavors with such, will be an acceptable service, as we have good grounds to hope the abundant reward of peace will attend our labors.

" I am, with true love,

" Thy real Friend,

" ISRAEL PEMBERTON."

At a meeting of the Treasurer and Trustees of the Friendly Association, held on the 5th of Tenth Month, 1758, there were present fourteen members. It was then agreed that those Friends who attend the forthcoming treaty, to be held at Easton, "may give any sum, not exceeding five hundred pounds, and do such other matters in our behalf as the occasion may require, and as if all the Trustees were present. James Pemberton, Joseph Richardson, Jacob Lewis, and Jacob Shoemaker, Jr., are appointed to get the goods together and forward them by wagon."

No other meeting occurs, until the 2d of Eleventh Month. During the interim, the treaty at Easton had taken place. The following minute is upon the book, relative to this subject:—"The clerk read the minutes of the Trustees who attended the late treaty at Easton, particularly, the manner in which they distributed the goods. James Pemberton, Jeremiah Warder, and Joseph Morris, are desired to examine and compare the quantities of goods given with what were procured, * * * * and also to adjust the accounts of the late expenses." Reference is then made to certain papers marked "A" and "B," for particulars of goods distributed, and minutes of the treaty, but after diligent search, these documents have not been found.

We learn from Charles Thomson, however, that there were present on that occasion, five hundred and one Indians, a few members of the Friendly Association, Governor Bernard of New Jersey, the Governor of Pennsylvania, Commissioners, interpreters, &c. Teedyuscung, who had increased his power and established himself as the head of five tribes, and the Chief Sachems of the Six Nations, were assembled—most of them—at George Croghan's house, near Easton, who appears to have been a mischief-maker, poisoning the minds of the Indians by misrepresentations and false-hoods, and at the same time poisoning their *blood*, by fire-water. This Croghan, had married the daughter of Nichos (a Mohawk chief), and his influence with the Indians, was largely owing to this fact.

The object of the treaty, seems to have been to re-duce the power of Teedyuscung, and to make him retract his statements concerning the fraud in pur-chases, made by the Proprietary agents. The attempt, however, proved a failure.

The conference was opened on the 8th of Tenth Month, by the usual compliments between the Govern-ors and the Indians. On the 10th and 11th, the In-dians remained in close consultation among themselves, whether what Teedyuscung had demanded at the last interview should now be insisted upon, or another proposition substituted. It was agreed, finally, to stand firm in the accusation of fraud and forgery on the part of the Proprietaries. The debates which ensued were warm, most of the chiefs assembled espousing the cause of Teedyuscung.

On the 11th, some of the Friends smoked a pipe with a few of the chiefs and old men of the several tribes, in attestation of their continued friendship. In the afternoon of that day, the conference was resumed, by the Governor of New Jersey welcoming the Indians in the name of his Province, and asserting his desire to do them justice, and live at peace ; but demanding as a token of their sincerity, that they surrender such prisoners among them, as were residents of New Jersey.

Teedyuscung then arose and said, they were met to

hear, and be heard. He reminded the Governor of Pennsylvania, of former complaints made against the Proprietaries, and of his willingness to do his part, towards securing a permanent peace.

Then Tagoshata, a Seneca chief, stated that, as the day was far spent, they had better adjourn until the morrow.

On the 12th they again met, but Teedyuscung made some disturbance, he being intoxicated. Tagoshata said, that through the advice of his people, the Minisinks and Delawares, had laid down the hatchet and were disposed to keep the peace. When the Indians finished their speeches, Isaac Norris, Speaker of the Assembly, told the Governors, he understood reports were being propagated among the Indians to his prejudice, and to set them against the people of this Province. He then called Moses Tetamie, a noted Indian, to declare whether he had heard among the Indians, that he, (Norris) had been concerned in the purchase of lands at or near Wyoming. But Tetamie declined to enter upon that matter now, as Teedyuscung was not in a condition to attend to business; whereupon Norris, who desired to return home, requested Tetamie to notify the Indians, that such reports were fabrications.

The next morning, before his departure, Isaac Norris had an interview with Teedyuscung, who told him that George Croghan had said, that he (Norris) and a Philadelphia Quaker, had been concerned with the New England people, in buying lands at Wyoming, which they had partially paid for, but had not satisfied the claim. Moreover, that Teedyuscung was urged by Croghan to say nothing at the treaty about the matter, for Croghan, as Commissioner for Sir William Johnson, would settle the Indians on these lands, notwithstanding this purchase. Teedyuscung, however, asserted their unwillingness to occupy the land, and their determination to resent the injury.

This conversation, induced Norris to sign a solemn declaration, which he presented to Teedyuscung, that the whole story was a groundless fabrication, and that neither he, nor any one for him, was concerned in the purchase of any land at or near Wyoming. This done, he sent for Croghan, and told him what the chief had said, which Croghan positively denied; but another Indian who was present confirmed Teedyuscung's story. Croghan asserted, that his diary contained exactly the words he had used, which he would show to the Governors at the proper time, but the Indians demanded that he produce it at once, which he declining to do, they reasonably concluded that Teedyuscung had spoken the truth.

On the 13th, Nichos made a speech, disclaiming Teedyuscung's authority, and seeking to influence the Indians against him.

On the 16th, the minutes of what had passed, were read. There was some wrangling among the Indians. The Munseys demanding the return of the belt by which they had put themselves and their affairs under the direction of the Six Nations, giving it to Teedyuscung.

On the 20th, the Council ended in confusion, as it was complained that the Mohawks had sold land belonging to the Delawares, amounting to about one and a half millions of acres. On the next day, Teedyuscung confirmed this sale for the sake of peace, but said this did not affect the claims he had formerly made, which he supposed had been referred to the determination of the King.

Tokubayo, a Cayuga chief, on this occasion, eulo-
gized Teedyuscung, and denounced the English. The
former he said spoke from the heart, the latter from
the lips. "If (said he) the English know not how to
manage Indian affairs, they should not call us together.
They have invited us here to brighten the chain of
peace, and have spent a fortnight disputing about
lands."

The treaty was concluded by an entertainment, after
which the chiefs were called together by R. Peters
and Conrad Weiser. Unfitted for business, owing to
their fondness for liquor, they were persuaded to sign
deeds, confirming previous purchases of valuable
lands by the Proprietaries, for which only a portion of
the consideration money had been paid, and which in
extent were far beyond the expectations of the Indians.
This laid the foundation for subsequent trouble.

Measures were taken at this treaty, by the Proprietary managers, not only to defraud the Indians out of
more land, but to set them, if possible, at variance with
each other. A member of the Friendly Association
says :—

" All our arguments, persuasions, and presents, were scarce sufficient to keep them from an open rupture. The business was shame-
fully delayed from day to day, which the minutes are calculated to
screen ; but it is well known to us who attended, that the time was
spent, in attempting Teedyuscung's downfall, and silencing or con-
tradicting the complaints he had made ; but he is really more of a
politician than any of his opponents, whether in or out of our Proprietary Council, and if he could be kept sober, might probably
soon become Emperor of all the neighboring nations."

Thus ended another disgraceful treaty, from which
we return to the records of the Friendly Association.
Under date of Eleventh Month 2d, the Trustees ordered

the payment of twenty dollars, to Moses Tetamie for his fidelity to the English, and his attention at treaties, whereat he seeks to cultivate peace with all the other Indians. A committee was appointed to answer the letter received from John Hunt and other English Friends, "and when done, to call a meeting so that the same may go by the next ship. The said committee, are desired to wait upon the Speaker of Assembly, and such other members as they may judge expedient, to know if they intend to collect and send to England the state of Indian affairs, and to reassure them, that if it is in the power of any of us, to furnish any original papers that may be wanting and useful, that we shall readily communicate them, and be of any further service in our power."

On the 11th of Eleventh Month the committee on an epistle, furnished one, which was read, and with some alterations approved.

"Israel Pemberton and the Clerk, are desired to have it copied fair, and after comparing it with the original, the Clerk is desired to sign it, and send it by one of the vessels now bound to London, and duplicate by the other vessel."

7th of Twelfth Month. The committee on accounts, reported progress and were continued.

"They are requested, when their work is completed, to call a meeting of the Trustees and Treasurer.

"The Clerk reports he had fair copies made of our letter to John Hunt and the other Friends in London ; that they were compared with the original, signed by him, and sent under cover to John Hunt, by Captains Patton and Hammitt.

"The distressed circumstances of some Indians who lately were at the Easton treaty being made known, it is agreed, that Isaac Zane, Peter Worrall, and Israel Pemberton, be a committee to administer to their necessities, in such manner as after inquiry, they may find best, with any sum not exceeding twenty pounds." Adjourned.

During this year the following Friends contributed to the funds of the Association, as appears from lists accompanying the "minute-book":—

City Subscribers.

	£	s.		£	s.
Matthias Aspden,	25	o	Deborah Claypoole,	50	o
Nathaniel Allen,	10	o	Thos. Coates, Jr.,	3	o
Nehemiah Allen,	5	o	Wm. Craige,	3	o
John Armitt,	20	o	Wm. Clifton,	5	o
Elizabeth Armitt,	3	o	John Cresson,	5	o
Wm. Atkinson,	2	o	Jonathan Cowpland,	5	o
James Arbuckle,	3	o	John Care,	3	o
Anonymous subscriptions,	39	o	Moore & Carpenter,	5	o
David Bacon,	5	o	David Deshler,	20	o
Davis Bassett,	3	o	Joseph Davis,	5	o
Joseph Baker,	10	o	Thos. Davis,	10	o
Anthony Benezet,	10	o	Henry Dennis,	5	o
Wm. Brown,	15	o	Susanna Dillwyn,	10	o
Nathan'l Brown,	5	o	John Drinker,	10	o
Thos. Brown, Jr.,	2	o	Jno. Drinker, Jr.,	5	o
Sam'l Bissell,	5	o	Henry Drinker,	10	o
John Bissell,	5	o	Joshua Emlen,	40	o
Sam'l Bryant,	5	o	Jeremiah Elfreth,	20	o
Jas. Bringhurst,	3	o	James Eddy,	10	o
Jno. Biddle,	10	o	Jonathan Evans,	5	o
John Bringhurst,	5	o	Cad'r Evans,	3	o
Sam'l Bonnell,	5	o	George Emlen, 5 pistoles		
Sam'l Bell,	3	o	per annum.		
Rich'd Blackman,	5	o	Joshua Fisher,	20	o
Thos. Clifford,	15	o	Wm. Fisher,	15	o
Jonathan Carmalt,	10	o	Solomon Fussell,	10	o
James Carmalt,	3	o	Henry Flower,	5	o
William Clark,	10	o	Joseph Galloway,	12	o
David Clark,	2	o	Jno. Guest,	3	o
Wm. Cooper,	25	o	Isaac Greenleafe,	20	o
Thomas Crosby,	50	o	Wm. Griffitts,	25	o
Wm. Callender,	25	o	Jno. Gillingham,	3	o
Abraham Carlile,	5	o	Sam'l Gusley,	10	o
Isaac Cathrall,	2	10	Ben. Gibbs, Jr.,	3	o

	£	s.		£	s.
Sam'l Griscomb,	5	8	Sam'l Massey,	7	0
Joshua Howell,	25	0	Joseph Marriott,	10	0
Benj. Hooten,	10	0	Thos. Maule,	30	0
Jno. Hatkinson,	10	0	Reese Meredith, per an.,	6	0
Jno. Hallowell,	3	0	Jonathan Miflin,	100	0
Joseph Hallowell,	2	0	Geo. Mifflin,	30	0
William Hinton,	2	0	John Miflin, Jr.,	10	0
Sam'l Head,	5	8	Benj. Miflin,	5	0
Susanna Head,	3	0	Sam'l Mickle,	5	0
Caleb Hawes,	3	0	Sam'l Miflin, Jr.,	5	8
Arent Hassert,	12	0	Benj. Marshall,	5	0
Rich. Humphries,	2	0	Wm. Morrison,	3	0
Eden Haydock,	5	0	John Morrison,	3	0
Rachel Hilburn,	2	0	George Morrison,	5	0
John Head,	10	0	William Moode,	12	0
Abel James,	25	0	Wm. Morris, Jr.,	10	0
James James,	5	0	Sam'l Morris, Jr.,	10	0
Joseph Jacob,	2	0	Joseph Morris,	25	0
Charles Jones,	25	0	Anthony Morris,	50	0
Owen Jones,	10	0	Anthony Morris, Jr.,	30	0
Edw. Jones,	5	0	Samuel Preston Moore,	20	0
Edw. Jones, Jr.,	2	0	Content Nicholson,	20	0
Aquilla Jones,	3	0	Sam'l Noble,	15	0
John Jones, merchant,	20	0	Sam'l Neave,	30	0
John Jones, shoemaker,	10	0	Sam'l Oldman,	10	0
Benjamin Kendall,	10	0	Dan'l Offley,	12	0
Jacob Lewis,	10	0	Patrick Ogilby,	4	0
Thos. Lightfoot,	10	0	Rich'd Parker,	10	0
Wm. Lightfoot,	10	0	Joseph Parker,	3	0
Samuel Lewis,	4	0	Robt. Parrish,	3	0
Henry Lisle,	5	0	John Parrock,	10	0
John Lyn,	10	0	Thos. Paschall,	5	0
Sarah Lyn,	3	0	Isaac Paschall,	5	0
Sally Lloyd,	5	0	Eliza Paschall,	15	0
James Lownes,	2	10	Beulah Paschall,	5	0
John Lownes,	5	8	Wm. Pearson,	5	0
Joseph Lownes,	3	0	Mary Peters,	1	10
D. Candry & N. Senior,	2	0	Joshua Pearson,	2	0
Benjamin Mason,	5	0	Israel Pemberton,	100	0
Abrah'm Mason,	4	0	John Pemberton,	100	0

	£	s.		£	s.
Jas. Pemberton,	50	0	Jacob Shoemaker, Jr.,	10	0
Sam'l Powell,	50	0	Thos. Shoemaker,	5	0
Mary Powell,	13	0	John Test,	5	0
Francis Rawle,	20	0	Christopher Thompson,	20	0
John Reynell,	100	0	Thos. Tillbury,	5	0
Peter Reeve,	15	0	Francis Trumble,	4	0
Jos. Richardson,	20	0	Jeremiah Warder,	50	0
Francis Richardson,	10	0	Robt. Waln,	15	0
Jos. Richardson,	16	0	Wm. West,	3	0
John Rich,	3	0	Chas. West, Jr.,	10	0
Sam'l Rhoads,	10	0	Sam'l Wetherill,	5	0
Hugh Roberts,	25	0	J. Jaggers and R. Webb,	3	0
Sam'l Sansom,	35	0	Catharine Wistar,	10	0
Jas. Saterthwaite,	5	0	Rich'd Wistar,	20	0
Thos. Say,	10	0	Jno. Wister,	20	0
Wm. Savery,	5	0	Ann and Thos. Wishart,	5	0
Joseph Saul,	3	0	Thos. Williams,	2	0
Wm. Shipley,	8	0	Wm. Wishart,	5	0
Henry Shute,	2	10	Dan'l Williams,	10	0
Rebecca Steele,	15	0	James Wood,	2	0
Mary Standley,	15	0	Richard Wood,	2	0
James Stephens,	3	0	Peter Worrall,	25	0
Stephen Stapler,	2	0	Isaac Zane,	50	0
Jacob Shoemaker,	15	0			

Total amount subscribed for the city in 1758, £2447 12s.

Abington.

	£	s.
Thomas Austin,	5	0
Abr'm Cadwallader,	2	10
Thos. Fletcher,	10	0
James Harker,	2	0
Rich'd Mather,	5	0
Joshua Morris,	20	0
Sam'l Parker,	1	10
James Paul,	8	0
Robert Paul,	5	0
Matthew Rea,	2	0
Thomas Wood,	1	0
Total,	£62	0

East Calne.

	£	s.
Joshua Baldwin,	3	0

Exeter and Maiden Creek.

	£	s.
Mordecai Ellis,	2	10
Morris Ellis,	2	0
Thomas Ellis,	2	0
Sam'l Embree,	2	10
David Ely,	3	0
Owen Hugh,	4	0
John Hughes,	5	0
Ellis Hughes,	2	10
Sam'l Hughes,	2	10

	£	s.
Wm. Iddings,	1	0
Benj. Lightfoot,	10	0
Jacob Lightfoot,	4	0
Mordecai Lee,	4	0
Samuel Lee,	3	0
Thomas Lee,	5	0
Joseph Millard,	3	0
Joseph Penrose,	5	0
William Penrose,	3	0
Conrad Price,	2	10
Job Pugh,	6	0
Michael Pugh,	3	0
Richard Penrose,	3	0
Francis Parvin,	10	0
Thomas Reed,	2	10
Moses Starr,	8	0
Michael Starr,	5	0
Moses Starr, Jr.,	1	0
John Scarlet,	2	0
Jacob Thomas,	3	10
Wm. Tomlinson,	3	0
Rob. Valentine,	10	0
Isaac Wickersham,	1	0
John Wells,	3	10
James Wood,	2	0

Germans not Friends.

	£	s.
John Bartlett,	4	0
Stephen Barnard,	3	0
Jacob Dexter,	1	0
Fred. Delaplank,	5	0
Christian Kinsey,	3	0
Abram Levan,	6	0
Jacob Levan,	10	0
Conrad Reiss,	2	10
Ellis Richt,	2	0
Jacob Weiss,	4	0
Total,	£170	10

Goshen.

	£	s.
Aaron Ashbridge,	10	0
George Ashbridge,	20	0
Joshua Baldwin,	2	0
Alexander Bane,	1	0
Ellis Davis,	5	0
Thos. Evans,	1	0
Isaac Haines,	2	0
Thos. Goodwyn,	3	0
Thos. Hoopes,	5	0
John Holland,	1	0
Benj. Hibberd,	5	0
Joseph James,	2	0
Rich'd Jones,	1	10
Nathan Lewis,	5	0
Nathan Matlack,	1	0
Randal Malin,	2	0
Thos. Milthouse, Jr.,	2	0
Wm. Starr,	1	10
George Smedley,	3	0
Rob. Valentine,	10	0
Amos Yarnall,	2	10
Amos Yarnall, Jr.,		10
Total,	£86	0

Gwynedd.

	£	s.
John Ambler,	2	0
Joseph Ambler,	5	0
Joseph Ambler, Jr.,	2	0
Robert Davis,		10
John Edwards,	5	0
Robert Edwards,	1	0
Abraham Evans,	2	10
Owen Evans,	10	0
Thomas Evans,	10	0
John Forman,	3	0
Thos. Foulke,	5	0
Wm. Foulke,	7	0
Amos Griffith,	3	0

	£	s.		£	s.
Hugh Griffith,	2	0	Ann Mendenhall,	2	10
Ellis Hughes,	1	10	Benj. Mendenhall,	5	0
Edw. Hughes,	5	0	Isaac Mendenhall,	5	0
Hugh Jones,	2	0	Sam'l Levis, Jr.,	5	0
Isaac Jones,	10	0	Lewis Lewis,	10	0
Jesse Jones,	3	0	Caleb Pierce,	5	0
John Jones,	5	0	Rob't Peirce,	4	10
Rob't Jones,	5	0	David Nichols,	5	0
Jacob Kashner,	3	0	Thos. Temple,	5	0
Abram Lukens,	5	0	Jacob Way,	5	0
Enos Lewis,	4	0	Jas. Wickersham,	2	10
Garret Peters,	2	0			
Eldad Roberts,	3	0	Total,	£107	05
John Roberts,	3	0			
John Roberts, Jr.,	5	0	*Nottingham.*		
Rob't Roberts,	15	0		£	s.
Jonathan Robeson,	2	10	James Brown,	10	0
Geo. Shoemaker,	1	0	Joshua Brown,	4	0
John Thomas,	1	10	George Churchman,	4	0
Rich'd Thomas,	2	0	John Churchman,	16	0
Dan'l Williams,	5	0			
John Williams,	3	0	Total,	£34	0
Abram Waggoner,	4	0			

	£	s.
Total,	£148	10

Kennett.

	£	s.
Joel Bailey,	5	0
Dan'l Bailey,	2	10
Thos Carleton,	10	0
Thos. Harlan,	5	0
David Hayes,	2	10
Amos Hope,	5	0
Amos Harvey,		5
Wm. Harvey,	10	0
Jacob Janney,	2	10
Wm. Levis,	5	0
Eliz'th Levis,	2	10
Ruth Mendenhall,	2	10

Plymouth.

	£	s.
John Bell,	2	10
Caleb Burne,	1	10
Andrew Cramer,	1	0
Barnabas Colson,	3	0
Geo. Castner,	5	0
Dennis Cunrad,	2	0
Henry Cunrad,	2	0
Sam'l Coulston,	1	10
Abram Davis,	20	0
John Davis,	2	0
Sam'l Davis,	7	0
Wm. Davis,	1	0
Joseph Dickenson,	1	0
John Delaplaine,	2	0
John Eastburne,	20	0
Rob't Eastburne,	3	0

	£	s.
Sam'l Evans,	2	10
Isaac Ellis,	2	0
Jos. Halwell,	3	0
John Jones,	5	0
Joseph Jones,	10	0
Wm. Lawrence,	3	0
Aaron Meredith,	5	0
John Morris,	30	0
Sam'l Morris,	20	0
Wm. Morris,	3	0
Peter Matson,	3	10
Merchant Maulsby,	1	10
David Morris,	2	0
Job Pugh,	6	0
Michael Pugh,	3	0
Wm. Robeson,	20	0
John Robinson,	1	10
John Rees,	2	0
Ellis Roberts,	1	0
Joseph Roberts,	6	0
Roger Roger,	2	10
James Stroud,	2	0
Wm. Stroud,	1	10
Edw. Stroud, Jr.,	3	0
Jonas Supplee,	2	0
Nathan Shepperd,	5	0
Joseph Trotter,	2	0
Joseph Waln,	15	0
James Wood,	2	0
Herman Yerkes,	2	0
Total,	£241	10

Providence.

	£	s.
John Calvert,	1	0
Cadwallader Evans,	3	0
Robert Evans,	2	0
Wm. Fell,	3	0
Jno. Fairlamb,	5	0

	£	s.
Rich'd Gorman,	1	5
Jno. Heacock,	1	10
Henry Howard,	3	0
George Miller,	25	0
John Minchall,	10	0
Thos. Minchall,	2	0
Sam'l Parke,	2	10
James Pennell,	3	0
Robert Pennell,	5	0
John Pennell, Jr.,	3	0
James Sharpless,	1	10
Sam'l Sharpless,	1	0
George Smedley,	2	10
Joshua Smedley,	2	10
Nathan Taylor,	2	10
Peter Taylor,	2	10
Jonathan Vernon,	1	0
Moses Vernon,	3	0
Nathan Yarnall,	3	0
Philip Yarnall,	2	10
Total,	£92	05

Richland.

	£	s.
Robert Ashton,	2	0
Thos. Adamson,	1	0
John Dennis,	5	0
Joseph Dennis,	1	0
Thos. Blackledge,	15	0
Wm. Edwards,	10	0
John Foulke,	2	0
Sam'l Foulke,	5	10
Theophilus Foulke,	2	0
Thomas Foulke,	1	0
William Heacock,	10	0
Lewis Lewis,	10	0
Morris Morris,	15	0
Rob't Penrose,	4	10
David Roberts,	1	0

	£	s.
Edw'd Roberts, ...	15	0
Abel Roberts, ...	8	0
Nathan Roberts, ...	1	10
Rich'd Roberts, ...	2	0
Thos. Roberts,.	5	10
Sam'l Shaw, ...		10
Edw'd Thomas, ...	2	0
John Thomas, ...	5	0
Thomas Thomas, ...	5	0
Total, ... £129		10

Springfield.

	£	s.
James Bartram, ...	15	0
Isaac Howell, ...	10	0
Total, ... £25		0

Westtown.

	£	s.
Jos. James, ...	2	0

Sadsbury and Lancaster.

	£	s.
Wm. Downing, ...	5	0
James Moore, ...	5	0
Thos. Poultney, ...	1	10
Caleb Steward,.	1	0
Isaac Whitelock, ...	15	0
Total, ... £27		10

West Calne, &c.

	£	s.	d.
Wm. Kirk, ...	1	1	9
Simon Meredith, . .	1	1	9
John Meredith, . . .	2	0	0
Thos. Martin, . . .		17	0
Total, ... £5		0	6

SUMMARY—1758.

	£	s.	d.		£	s.	d.
City, ...	2,477	12	0	Providence, . .	92	5	0
Abington, . . .	62	0	0	Richland, . . .	129	10	0
East Calne, . .	3	0	0	Sadsbury, &c., .	27	10	0
Exeter, &c., . .	170	10	0	Springfield,. . .	25	0	0
Goshen, ...	86	0	0	Westtown, . . .	2	0	0
Gwynedd, . . .	148	10	0	West Calne, . .	5	0	6
Kennett,. . . .	107	5	0				
Nottingham, . .	34	0	0	Grand total, £3,611		12	6
Plymouth, . . .	241	10	0	About $10,000.			

At the meeting on the 4th of First Month, 1759, no business transpired of interest. The committee reported they forwarded a letter to Israel Pemberton.

On the 23d of same month, it was announced that—

"Thomas King, Totienonah, Shackalamy, and several other Indians in the British interest, are come to town from the westward. Richard Wistar, Isaac Zane, Jacob Shoemaker, and the Clerk, are desired to converse with them, and if they are in want of clothing or other necessaries, to make them presents on account of the Friendly Association.

"Thomas Say, Richard Wistar, and James Pemberton, are desired forthwith to join Israel Pemberton, William Callender, and Abel James in revising the minutes of this Association, to be sent to our friends in England.

"In consideration of the late eminent services of Frederic Post, in going of messages for the government into the Indian country, and conducting therein with integrity in promoting the good work of peace, it is agreed, that the Treasurer do pay him out of the fund of this Association, the sum of twenty-five pounds. Also agreed, that the Treasurer do pay the sum of five pounds to William Hayes, he having accompanied the said Frederic Post, on one of his journeys, and conducted, from all we have heard, very well." Adjourned.

Although not pertaining *strictly* to the affairs of the Friendly Association, it is worthy of note, that on the 13th of this month "the Meeting for Sufferings" sent an address to Governor Denny, vindicating Friends, from malicious charges, of seeking to injure the reputation of the Proprietaries by unduly influencing the Indians to complain of frauds, &c. The following is a copy of the address :—

"*To William Denny, Esq., Lieutenant-Governor of the Province of Pennsylvania, and the Council of the said Province :*

"The address of the Meeting for Sufferings of the people called Quakers, in the said Province and New Jersey, respectfully sheweth, that we have seriously considered the answer given by the Governor the 10th instant to our address, presented on the 14th of last month, and believe it to be our duty, in justice to ourselves and our Friends whom we are appointed to represent, now to renew our request to the Governor and his Council, to favor us with a copy of the report of the committee of Council, appointed by the Governor to inquire into the complaints of the Indians at the Treaty at Easton, ye 8th Nov., 1756, and we humbly desire our address may be again considered and our request granted, that we may have an opportunity of vindicating ourselves from the aspersions cast on us, and of giving a true account of our conduct and proceedings in the late negotiations of this Government with the Indians, by which we have no doubt of being able to obviate any cause for objections thereto, and making it evident to our superiors and all others, that we have acted through the course of our transactions, in the fear of God, with loyalty to our gracious King, and a most sincere concern, to put a stop to the ravages, distresses, and bloodshed, which prevail on our frontier inhabitants, and to promote the real interest and peace of our country.

"We are the more earnestly engaged to urge this request, as we have received undoubted intelligence from our Friends in London, that though the name of our religious society may not be expressly mentioned in the said report of Council, yet it evidently appears to be designed to lay on us, the whole blame of the late Indian ravages, as a paragraph of the said report communicated to us, is to the following effect :—' We cannot but impute the said Teedyuscung's making the base charge of forgery against the Proprietaries, to the malicious suggestions and management of some wicked people, enemies to the Proprietaries, and perhaps it would not be unjust in us, if we were to impute it to some of those busy, forward people, who, in disregard of the express injunctions of his Majesty's Ministers, it and your Honors repeated notices thereof served on them, would nevertheless appear in such crowds at the late Indian Treaties, and there shew themselves so busy and active, in the management and support of the Indians, in those complaints against the Proprietaries.'

"We are conscious of our innocence, and that we are not justly chargeable with any act, to the injury of the Proprietaries of this Province, either in their reputation or interest ; and it is now too generally known here, to need any proof to be offered, that many of us, have used our endeavors as far as we could, consistent with our stations and a due regard to the Government under which we live, for the restoring and confirming the peace of the Province ; but as the insinuations of our influencing the Indians to complain of injustice and fraud committed by the Proprietaries or their agents, are made use of, to render us obnoxious to our superiors in England, we are desirous of receiving from the Governor and Council, the whole of these charges, in such manner that we may acquit ourselves, and by manifesting the integrity of our principles and practices, prevent the injuries which by this private attack on our characters, seem to be intended against our interest and reputation as a Religious Society.

"As the Governor on a former occasion, gave us assurance that he would countenance and protect us in our religious and civil rights and liberties, and that no act should be done during his administration, by which either of them should be affected, without our being heard in our own justification, we therefore desire the Governor and Council, will on this interesting occasion, grant us a full copy of the said report of Council, &c., and thereby indulge us with the common rights of Englishmen, of being heard, before we are condemned.

" If the Proprietaries were here, we should make our application to them, agreeable to the Governor's directions ; but as it is not practicable to do it without defeating our intention of doing ourselves justice in a proper way and time, we desire the Governor and Council, may not be displeased with this application, but may give it the most charitable construction, and grant this our reasonable request.

" Signed by appointment and on behalf of our said meeting, held at Philadelphia, 13th First Month, 1759."

On the 1st of Second Month, appears the following minute :—

" Our friends, Hugh Roberts and Anthony Benezet, attended this meeting, with a request from the 'Meeting for Sufferings' desiring, that we would furnish Friends in England, with such minutes of our proceedings in the business we have been engaged in, in promoting a pacification with the Indians, as may demonstrate the injustice of the charges contained against us in the report of the Governor's Council sent to London, some time since to the Proprietaries, and handed about in order to reproach us, and the Society of Friends, which is particularly recommended to the care of the Committee appointed to that service."

The committee on accounts, reported at the meeting on the 1st of Third Month, that the Association was indebted to sundry persons to an amount, aggregating three hundred and forty-one pounds fourteen shillings six pence, and orders were drawn on the Treasurer for that sum. It was agreed at this meeting, to pay Moses Tetamie five pounds "when Israel Pemberton may judge it will be most useful to him." There being a few Conywaga Indians in the city, the standing Committee was authorized to furnish them with needed things, to an amount not exceeding twelve pounds.

The following agreement I find under this date:—

"WHEREAS, A brigade of horses are raised by Sam'l Lightfoot, of Chester county, for the use of Israel Pemberton, to convey goods and stores to Pittsbourg, and hath nominated, appointed, and constituted Thomas Kinton of Monahan, in the county of York, Master of said brigade, authorizing him to exercise, do and perform the authority, duty and service of packhorse-master over the said brigade, if no casualty prevents ;—

"Now it is hereby witnessed, that we, Joseph Wright, John Mickle, Jr., James Hammond, Patrick Quin, Christian Miller, have agreed with the said Sam Lightfoot, to undertake, do, and perform the office, duty, and service of drivers of packhorses ; that is to say, each of us shall, and will take the care, oversight, and charge of six of said horses, if so many are committed to us or any of us. And we do each of us hereby promise, and agree, faithfully, and honestly to perform the duty and service of pack-horse-drivers, according to the best of our skill and ability, and duly observe the directions and instructions of the said Thomas Kinton, or whom the said Israel Pemberton shall appoint as pack-horse-master, in all his proper and reasonable commands, until we are discharged out of this service.

"In consideration of which service, thus performed, the said Sam Lightfoot, in behalf of the said Israel Pemberton, doth hereby covenant, promise, and agree, to find and provide for each of the said drivers, one matchcoat, and one blanket, if needed, and suitable and sufficient provision of meat and drink, and pay unto each of them, three shillings lawful money, for each day during their continuance in the said service.

"For the true performance of which agreement, we have hereunto interchangeably set our hands, this first day, of the Third Month, A. D. 1759, in the county of York.

"And further, it is hereby agreed by the said parties, that any of the said drivers, shall have their discharge, at any time on giving suitable notice, so as not to discommode the said Pemberton or his agent.

"JOSEPH WRIGHT,
"JAMES HAMMOND,
"JOHN MICKLE, Jr.,
"CHRISTIAN (C M) MILLER,
"PATRICK (P Q) QUIN.

In presence of—

WILLIAM BEALS,
JAMES HAMMEL.

"*By John Forbes, Esq., Brigadier-General of his Majesty's forces, Colonel of the Seventeenth Regiment of foot, and commanding his Majesty's forces in the Southern Provinces of North America, &c., &c., &c.*

"WHEREAS, A power and authority is given by me, to Israel Pemberton, to carry to Pittsburg such Indian goods as he has upon hand, to traffick with Indians upon just and equitable terms, and under the eye and direction of the commanding officer, at Pittsbourg (now Colonel Mercer), there.

"Wherefore, all commanding officers of his Majesty's forces, as well as those of the Provinces, are hereby directed and required, to give all aid and assistance, in the safe conduct of the above stores unto Israel Pemberton, or whom he shall appoint as commissary for carrying the said goods to Pittsbourgh; and the commanding officers of forts and garrisons, are by no means, to suffer any men or horses employed in this service, to be carried away, or any ways stopt in doing their duty, either in going from ye inhabited parts to Pittsbourgh, or in their return home. The commanding officer at Pittsbourgh, is hereby required and directed, to give all aid and assistance to Israel Pemberton or his commissary, in building stores, escortes,

&c., for the preservation and protection of the goods, and take particular care, that in the sale and barter of their goods, they conform to the prices and regulations fixed by the Provincial Commissioners, to prevent confusion in the trade.

"Given under my hand, at the Three Tuns, this 15th January, 1759.

"JO. FORBES.

"To all officers concerned.

"Brigadier-General Forbes, having been pleased to grant the within powers, respecting the Indian trade, to Mr. Israel Pemberton of Philadelphia, these, are to confirm and continue the same, of which all officers, civil and military, are to take notice, and regulate their conduct accordingly.

"Given at Philadelphia this fourth day of April, 1759.

"JOHN STANWIX."

It appears from a letter of Israel Pemberton, that he sent some two thousand pounds' worth of goods to Pittsburg, where a treaty was to be held, between the Indians and General Forbes, then stationed at Fort Pitt. The money contributed to this object, came largely from the Germans; the balance, was from his private purse. There is no mention of this liberal donation, upon the books of the Association.

On 9th of Fourth Month, a Committee was appointed, to collect in such accounts against the Association, as remained unpaid, and to prepare a full statement of its financial condition, to be laid before the General Meeting on the 19th.

"Joseph Morris, Jacob Lewis, Owen Jones, and James Pemberton, are to give notice of the General Meeting, to be held on the 19th, at ten o'clock, at Friends' Schoolhouse, to all the contributors below Chestnut street. Isaac Zane, Jacob Shoemaker, and Jeremiah Warder, are to notify contributors between Chestnut and Arch Streets, and William Callender, Thomas Say, and the Clerk, undertake to notify contributors in town above Arch street, as well as those that live in the Northern Liberties. Israel Pemberton, is requested to write some of the principal contributors in each neighborhood in the country, that all may be reminded of the time of our General Meeting. Israel Pemberton, Owen Jones, and Isaac Zane, are appointed to wait upon General Amherst, now in this city, to acquaint him with the motives which induced Friends of this Province, to enter into this Association, and of our past conduct and present views."

On the 16th of Fourth Month, the committee on accounts, reported that the Association owed to various persons, eighty-three pounds eighteen shillings and nine pence, and orders were drawn on the Treasurer, canceling the indebtedness. Space is left for the report of the committee who waited upon General Amherst, which I have been unable to find.

At the General Meeting, on the 19th of Fourth Month, 1759, the following Trustees and Treasurer, were chosen by ballot:—

Israel Pemberton, Thomas Say, James Pemberton, Jacob Lewis, Isaac Zane, Hugh Roberts, Owen Jones, Jeremiah Warder, Isaac Howell, Abel James, Jonathan Mifflin, George Miller, Joshua Morris, Abraham Dawes, Charles West, Jr., and Jacob Shoemaker, Jr., Trustees, and for Treasurer, John Reynell. Obligations were given as heretofore, for the faithful performance of their trust.

It was agreed to meet hereafter, at Alexander Seaton's, on the Fifth day of the first week in every month, at three o'clock, P. M., or more frequently, if deemed necessary by Israel Pemberton, Isaac Zane, Jeremiah Warder, Jacob Shoemaker, Jr., and the Clerk. These Friends, were authorized to perform such "lesser services as may occur, which will not involve calling all the Trustees together."

On the 16th of Seventh Month, Israel Pemberton acquainted the meeting that General Stanwix had desired him "to purchase and get ready to be forwarded towards Pittsburg, (late Fort Du Quesne) a large quantity of goods suitable for clothing and other uses of the Indians, that may come to that place, to be given them at the expense of the British Government, to promote peace, and confirm the Indians that way in the British interest," &c. It was deemed very desirable to forward these goods with the utmost dispatch, and Israel Pemberton, Hugh Roberts, Jacob Shoemaker, Jr., and Abel James, were appointed to make enquiry concerning the matter, and call a meeting whenever it was deemed necessary.

On the 2d of Eighth Month, the above Committee reported, that goods bought by Israel Pemberton, had been "sent towards Pittsburg, by persons that have voluntarily engaged in carrying them up at a small additional expense, over the customary rates paid by the government."

On the 4th of Tenth Month, William Shipley presented an account, for two dozen dried tongues furnished Isaac Zane for his journey to Wyoming, amounting to forty-eight shillings, which the Treasurer is desired to "discount in settling his subscription." Friends were notified that a lad about sixteen years old, had just been released from captivity by some Indians, and brought into Shamokin. A committee was appointed "to get him some learning and clothing, at the expense of this Association." Also, to furnish Abraham Locquies, "an ancient Indian, with clothing or any other acceptable present, he being about to go to Wyoming to his children." Also, to supply "Teedyuscung and some other Indians, now in town, with necessaries. The whole not to exceed twenty pounds in value."

On the 1st of Eleventh Month, the committee reported that the lad above mentioned had been taken by the Commissioners for the Indian trade into their service.

On the 6th of Twelfth Month, a minute states :—

"Two Indian messengers being in this city from Alleghany, and also present at this meeting, who are charged with messages to the westward to several of the Indian natives on the branches of the Susquehanna, in order to bring about a general treaty between the Indians and this and adjacent Provinces next summer, therefore, it is agreed, that Israel Pemberton, Isaac Zane, Isaac Howell, and Jacob Shoemaker, Jr. be a committee, to assist in getting them furnished by the Provincial Commissioners, with such things as they may want, and to contribute thereto, out of the fund of this Association, any sum not exceeding twenty-five pounds. And said committee may furnish Teedyuscung, with such things as they may judge necessary, not exceeding twenty-five pounds value, to promote and assist his continuing his care in bringing in more captives, (he having now brought in four), as also to enable and encourage him to attend such treaties amongst the Indians, where his personal attendance may be beneficial to the affairs of these Provinces, and the British interest."

"On the 20th of Twelfth Month, the committee informed they had given 'Tingoqua and the other Indian messengers lately come to town, four strouds, four matchcoats, a brass kettle, four thousand black, and four thousand white wampum, besides sundry lesser articles, which he handsomely acknowledged the receipt of. And that they gave Teedyuscung, six strouds, six matchcoats, and three thousand wampum, which he in like manner acknowledged the receipt of, by thanking the Quakers for them, and went out of town well satisfied.'

"It having often been under the solid consideration of the Trustees and Treasurer of this Association, whether it might not tend to promote the services in which we have been engaged, to address the Proprietaries of this Province, and to write John Hunt and some other of our Friends in London, informing them of the present situation of Indian affairs, and what appears to us just, and absolutely serviceable to be done, in order to have peace with the Indians and British colonies settled on a lasting foundation.— It is now agreed that Israel Pemberton, Hugh Roberts, Isaac Zane, and the Clerk be a committee, to make essays of them, and when done, to call a meeting."

First Month 3d, 1760. Isaac Zane presented his account, amounting to forty pounds eighteen shillings six pence, which was paid.

Second Month 7th, 1760. At this meeting it was reported that "there are powers lately come from the Proprietaries, to make the Indians reasonable satisfaction, for their claims respecting lands. Accordingly, Israel Pemberton, Isaac Zane, and the Clerk, were appointed to wait upon the Governor; and John Reynell, Owen Jones, and Hugh Roberts to wait upon William Logan, or any others, from whom it may be likely to obtain intelligence concerning this matter. Said committees, having power to call a meeting to deliberate further thereon."

These Committees, made report on the 14th of Second Month, that Governor Hamilton had authority from the Proprietaries, to settle all matters in dispute about lands on the Delaware River, as mentioned at the Easton treaty, and that he would seek to do so, at the earliest opportunity. William Logan confirmed this statement of the Governor. Nevertheless, the Committee appointed to address the Proprietaries, were continued.

On the 21st of Second Month, they reported progress. Information was given at this meeting, that the Assembly had ordered the printing of some Indian treaties for distribution. Whereupon Israel Pemberton and the Clerk, were directed to inquire of some members of Assembly "what number it is proposed to have printed," and to encourage that body to issue "such a number, as may admit Friends and others, generally to have them."

On the 18th of Third Month, "An essay of an address to the Proprietaries was read, considered, and after some alterations and additions approved." The Committee were requested, to make an essay of a letter to John Hunt and John Fothergill, to accompany said address, and to have two fair copies made, and to call a meeting to consider the essay, and sign the address.

On the 20th of Third Month, two fair copies of the letter and the address were read, approved, and signed by all present. Israel Pemberton forwarded the same.

On the 3d of Fourth Month, 1760, committees were appointed to notify contributors in the city and country of the General Meeting to take place on the 19th inst.

Thomas Say and Charles West, Jr. were to inform those contributors living above Arch street.

Hugh Roberts, Owen Jones, and Jeremiah Warder, those between Arch and Market streets.

Jacob Shoemaker and Isaac Howell, those between Market and Chestnut streets.

Jacob Lewis and James Pemberton, those contributors residing below Chestnut street.

Abraham Dawes, those in his neighborhood, and Israel Pemberton, to notify some of the principal contributors in different country neighborhoods.

Committees were also appointed, to examine and prepare the minutes of last year, as also a financial statement to be laid before the General Meeting.

"Inasmuch as Teedyuscung, Moses Tetamie, and some other Indians were to accompany Frederic Post and

John Hayes, as messengers from this Government, to Indians on the Ohio, a Committee of four Friends, were appointed to confer with the Provincial Commissioners, and ascertain if this Association can be serviceable in fitting them out for the journey, and were authorized to contribute a sum, not exceeding fifty pounds, to this end."

On the 10th of Fourth Month, this Committee reported, that they had agreed to contribute to the expenses of the journey. They stated, also, that Moses Tetamie desired Friends to take some notice of his daughter during his absence; and a Committee of four Friends were appointed, "to get her boarded in a reputable house, where she may have the advantage of some schooling."

On the 19th of Fourth Month, the Committee appointed to examine the Treasurer's accounts state :—

"That since the adjustment of accounts last year, he hath received from sundry members of this Association, the sum of £443 11s. 6d., which with the balance of £41 19s. 4d. remaining in his hands last year, amounts to £485 4s. 10d., and, that he hath paid, in pursuance of orders and direction of the Trustees, £238 0s. ½d., being the amount of all accounts brought in, so that there now remains in his hands £247 4s. 9½d. The general state of the accounts being prepared, all the managers present agreed to attend with them at the General Meeting immediately, and lay them before such Committee as may be there appointed, to examine and adjust the same."

* * * * * * * * * * * * * *

Here endeth the "minute-book," and the continuity of this narrative.

Precisely when this useful organization closed its labors, has long been a matter of doubt, some claiming that it was in existence as late as 1767, but upon what evidence does not appear.

In a work entitled "North American Indians and Friends," published by the Aborigines Committee of the Meeting for Sufferings (London, 1844), it is stated (page 91) that the "Friendly Association" continued until "*the time of the definitive treaty of 1764.*" In the absence of better authority, the above should be regarded as the correct date.

The condition of the Indian tribes, during the "seven years'" war, was characteristically described by a chief, who said to an Englishman, "You and the French, are like the two edges of a pair of shears. We, are the cloth, which is cut to pieces between them." They sued for peace, and the stipulations demanded, were complied with in 1764. General Gage, congratulates Lord Halifax, under date of "December 13th," (this year), "that the country is restored to its former tranquillity, and that a general and, it is hoped, lasting peace is concluded with all the Indian nations who have taken up arms against his Majesty."

These facts, are confirmatory of the statement, that as an organized body, the "Friendly Association" ceased to exist at or near the date of the "definitive treaty" above mentioned. Moreover, about this time also, the Indians, from various causes, moved westward in large numbers.

In 1773, Zebulon Heston and John Parrish, traveled some four hundred and fifty miles from Philadelphia, (beyond the Ohio), to visit the Indians. (See Appendix for Epistles they carried with them.) It was through the labors of the "Friendly Association" that our Religious Society, was brought to see the necessity of using its powerful influence, *officially*, to shelter the too-confiding Indians. The present Committees on Indian Affairs appointed by the various Yearly

Meetings throughout this country, are so many scions from this parent stem.

In 1792, when the Indians and this Government were at war, the *Yearly Meeting* " nominated a large Committee, to unite with the *Meeting for Sufferings*, to endeavor to promote a termination of hostilities." To this end they "memorialized the President and Congress."

In 1795, the Committee " for promoting the improvement and gradual civilization of the Indian Natives," was appointed by the Yearly Meeting of Pennsylvania, New Jersey, &c. They sent letters to the various Tribes, with one "from the Secretary of State, expressive of the approbation of the Executive Government," &c., and soon thereafter commenced their civilizing and Christianizing work, by sending suitable Friends to live among them. (See Appendix for names of above Committee, &c.)

From this date the Yearly Meetings, have had the Indians under their care.

In conclusion, I would state, that the preparation of this history of the Friendly Association, (which I believe to be more full than any preceding one, embracing about four years of its existence,) has been a pleasing task. And whereas, one hundred and twenty years ago, the then little colony of Pennsylvania, through its political machinery, sought to overthrow the Association whose history we have been considering ; in our day, a great Nation, through its chosen head, seeks the council and aid, of those who can rightfully claim religious fellowship with the members of the Friendly Association, to promote the work of peace with Indians, which they commenced.

APPENDIX.

---·---

BOND OF THE TRUSTEES OF THE FRIENDLY ASSOCIATION.

KNOW ALL MEN BY THESE PRESENTS, That we, Israel Pemberton, Isaac Zane, Jacob Lewis, Charles West, Junr., Abel James, James Pemberton, Jeremiah Warder, David Deshler, Joshua Howell, Thomas Say, William Lightfoot, Jacob Shoemaker, Junr., Isaac Howell, George Miller, Abraham Dawes, and Francis Rawle Trustees chosen by the General Meeting of the members of the Friendly Association for regaining and preserving peace with the Indians by pacific measures, are held and firmly bound unto Jeremiah Elfreth, Richard Parker, Benjan Hooten, Owen Jones, Isaac Greenleafe, Jacob Shoemaker, Senr., Anthony Benezet, Henry Drinker, Robert Parrish, John Drinker, Junr., Daniel Offley, Joseph Jacob, all of the city of Philadelphia, Joshua Morris, of Abington, Thomas Evan, of Gwynnedd, Samuel Foulke, of Richland, Bucks county, and Aaron Ashbridge, of Goshen, Chester county, members of said Association, and to the survivors or survivor of them, and to their, or his assigns, in the sum of two thousand pounds lawful money of Pennsylvania, to be paid to the said Jeremiah Elfreth, Richard Parker, Benjamin Hooten, Owen Jones, Isaac Greenleafe, Jacob Shoemaker, Senr., Anthony Benezet, Henry Drinker, Robert Parrish, John Drinker, Junr., Daniel Offley, Joseph Jacob, Joshua Morris, Thomas Evan, Samuel Foulke, and Aaron Ashbridge, and the survivors or survivor of them, their certain attorney or assigns, to the which payment well and truly to be made and done, we do bind ourselves, our heirs, executors, administrators, and every of them severally but not jointly, nor one of us for the act of the others. Seal'd with our seals, dated the twenty-first day of the Fifth Month, called May, in the first year of the reign of King George the Third, and in the year of our Lord one thousand seven hundred and sixty-one.

The condition of this obligation is such, that if the above
bounden Israel Pemberton, Isaac Zane, Jacob Lewis, Charles West,
Junr., Abel James, James Pemberton, Jeremiah Warder, David
Deshler, Joshua Howell, Thomas Say, William Lightfoot, Jacob
Shoemaker, Junr., Isaac Howell, George Miller, Abraham Dawes,
and Francis Rawle, as Trustees of the said Friendly Association,
keep fair minutes of their resolutions and proceedings, and render
a just and true account of all sums of money contributed by the
members of the said Association, and entrusted with the said Trustees, and shall at the time of the next general election of Trustees,
or at any other time, when thereunto required by the General
Meeting of the members of the said Association, render and sub-
mit their said minutes and accounts to the examination of such
committee or committees, as may be appointed or chosen by the
said General Meeting, and by proper vouchers, prove that the several sums contributed for the service of the said Association and
entrusted with them, are or have been applied to the uses and purposes thereby intended, agreeable to the rules and articles made
by the said General Meeting for that end, and no part thereof to
the private use or service of the said Trustees, nor of any of them;
and if they shall in all things well and truly fulfill, observe, and
keep the rules, articles, and agreements concluded and agreed
upon by the General Meeting of the members of the said Association, without claiming, retaining, or receiving any fee, gratuity, or
reward whatsoever, then this obligation to become void; otherwise
to be and remain, in full force and virtue.

Joshua Howell,	[L. S.]	Isaac Zane,	[L. S.]
Thos. Say.	[L. S.]	Jere'ah Warder,	[L. S.]
Wm. Lightfoot,	[L. S.]	Chars. West, Junr.,	[L. S.]
Jacob Shoemaker, Jr.,	[L. S.]	Abel James,	[L. S.]
Isaac Howell,	[L. S.]	James Pemberton,	[L. S.]
Abraham Dawes,	[L. S.]	Jacob Lewis,	[L. S.]
Isaac Greenleafe,	[L. S.]	David Deshler.	[L. S.]
Isr. Pemberton,	[L. S.]		

Sealed and delivered by Israel Pemberton, Isaac Zane, Charles
West, Junior, Abel James, James Pemberton, David Deshler, Wm.
Lightfoot, Jacob Shoemaker, Jr., and Isaac Howell in presence of—

William Beder,
Alexr. Seaton.

Sealed and delivered by Jer. Warder and Thos. Say, in presence of—

> THOS. CANBY,
> JOS. FOX.

Sealed and delivered by Jacob Lewis, in presence of—

> ROBT. LEWIS, JUNR.,
> JOHN REYNELL.

Sealed and delivered the 29th Seventh Month, 1761, by Isc. Greenleafe and Abm. Dawes, in the presence of—

> JOHN ELLIOTT,
> ISAAC LOBDELL.

Sealed and delivered by Josa. Howell, in presence of—

> ALEXR. SEATON,
> MOSES PATTERSON.

———

CERTIFICATE OF MEMBERSHIP IN THE FRIENDLY ASSOCIATION.

Philadelphia, 11th Day of 2nd Month, 1758

THIS is to certify, that *John Pemberton* of *the City of Philadelphia Merchant,* hath contributed the Sum of *One Hundred Pounds* to the *Friendly Affociation for regaining and preferving Peace with the* Indians *by pacifick Meafures,* and is thereby become one of the Members of faid *Friendly Affociation.*

John Reynell Treafurer.

A LIST OF PAPERS SENT TO JOHN HUNT, PER THE "CAROLINA," SIXTH MONTH 18th, 1758.

A.—Description of the old town of Wyoming, in 1743.

B.—Copy of C. Weiser's minutes of conversations with Indians at Fort Allen, November 20th, 1757.

C.—Intelligence from Susquehanna, April 23d, 1758.

D.—Intelligence from Susquehanna, May 20th, 1758.

E.—Minutes of Conferences, between Governor of Pennsylvania and Teedyuscung, April 29th to May 5th, 1758.

F.—Teedyuscung's message, by his two sons, to the Ohio Indians, April 10th, 1758.

G.—Indian intelligence from Bethlehem, June 1st, 1758.

H.—Minutes of Friendly Association, &c., 20th Fifth Month, 1758, with account of I. Zane's going to Wyoming, &c.

I.—Letter from I. Zane, at Wyoming, 29th Fifth Month, 1758.

K.—Message from the Cherokees to the Delawares.

L. M.—Copy of message, sent by Governor of Pennsylvania, June 7th, 1758, to Teedyuscung and the Delawares at Wyoming, and to the Indians on the head of the Susquehanna, and its branches.

N.—Copy of instructions from the Governor of Pennsylvania, to Charles Thomson and Frederick Post, messengers sent to Teedyuscung, &c., June 7th, 1758.

O.—Conferences between Teedyuscung and messengers from Governor of Pennsylvania, &c., at Nescopuck, June 12th, 1758.

P.—C. Thomson and C. F. Post's Report, &c., to the Governor and General Forbes.

Q.—Copy of a letter to John Hunt, Fifth Month, 31st.

R.—Message from the Cherokees to the Six Nations.

S.—Journal of F. Post, Commissioner sent to Wyoming.

T.—Journal of Moses Tetamie, sent to Minisink Indians.

U.—Minutes of Conferences with Indians at Philadelphia, July, 1758. The Penn *Gazette* of July, 1758. Copy of letter to J. Hunt by the Packet, Sixth Month 29th, 1758.

CERTIFICATE TO ZEBULON HESTON AND JOHN LACY.

" *To the Indians living to the westward of the Province of Pennsylvania, or any others among whom this writing may come :*

"The Friends, called Quakers, assembled at their Monthly Meeting, in Wrightstown, in the County of Bucks in Pennsylvania, the sixth day of the Seventh Month, in the year of our Lord 1773, saluteth with love.

" The Great Spirit above, who created the world, and man to inhabit it, having put into the heart of our beloved friend and brother Zebulon Heston, to pay you a visit in the love of our Lord and Saviour Jesus Christ, we hereby inform you, that he is a brother who has long lived amongst us, is of a good life and conversation, and we think, has been called by this Great Spirit, to give religious advice and instruction to us, and others. And we much desire that it may please the same Great Spirit, to be with him in his travels, and enable him to perform his religious duty among you, and that your hearts may be opened to feel what he may say to you, to be good, and lead you to attend to the dictates of the Divine Spirit 'in your own hearts, which will make you good men in this world, and when you die, you will then live with that Great Spirit forever.

"We also think it necessary to inform you, that our brother Zebulon Heston, being an old man, there comes a young man with him, to be assistant to him in his long journey. His name is John Lacy. (He) is of a sober life, and well esteemed by us.

"We recommend them both to the protection of the Great Almighty Being, whom we profess to worship, and desire the Indians to be kind and loving towards them.

" Signed in and on behalf of our said Monthly Meeting, by

" JOSEPH CHAPMAN,	THOMAS ROSS,
WM. CHAPMAN,	DAVID BUCKMAN,
JNO. WILKINSON.	WM. LEE,
JOSEPH SMITH,	ABR'M CHAPMAN,
JNO. HIRST, .	JOHN TERREY,
BENJAM'N WIGGINS,	JOHN BEAUMONT,
ROBT. HILLBOURNE,	THOS. HILLBOURN,
STEPHEN TWINING,	WM. ATKINSON,
JOHN TERREE, JUNR.,	MOSES SMITH,
WM. SMITH,	JOSEPH HELLBOURNE,

BENJAM'N CHAPMAN,
HAMPTON WILSON,
ROBERT VEREE,
JOSEPH WHITE,
JOHN LACEY ELDER,
THOS. WHITSON,
JOSH. MORRISSON,
SAML. SMITH,
ISAAC KIRKE,
THOMAS BETTS,
JOHN HAMPTON,
JOHN STOCDALE,
JOHN WARNER,

BENJAM'N HAMPTON,
SAM'L EASTBURN,
ISAAC WIGGINS,
JOSEPH STRADLING,
ISAAC SMITH,
JNO. WATSON, JUNR.,
STEPHEN SMITH,
JOHN WARNER, JUNR.,
JOHN HELME,
THOS. ATKINSON,
WM. SMITH,
JOSEPH HAMPTON,
ISSACHAR MORRIS."

CERTIFICATE TO JOHN PARRISH.

"To the Indians to the westward of Pennsylvania, or whom this may concern, Greeting:

"The Great and Good Spirit above, who is the only true God, the Maker and Creator of all things, and who made mankind to dwell upon the earth, loveth them and would have them love, serve, and worship Him that they may be happy here, and when they die and go out of this world, they may go up to Him, and there be always happy, and at rest, and die no more.

"This Great, Good, and Holy Spirit, having, as we believe, put it into the heart of our dear friend, Zebulon Heston, to visit some of the Indian tribes to the westward of this Province, in love and good-will, in order that they may be taught and instructed to love, serve, obey, and worship the only true, holy, God, who hath placed in the hearts of all men a principle or Good Spirit, that shews unto them, good and evil;—and the same Good Spirit having put it into the heart of our friend, John Parrish, in love and good-will to accompany our friend Zebulon Heston, in his intended visit to the Indians, we desire they may be rec'd in love, and that the Good Spirit may open your ears and your hearts, to hear and understand what they may have to say for your good, and instruction. We are glad that the Great God, hath moved upon the hearts of these, our friends, to make you this religious visit. They are true men, and love the Indians, and tho' we do not, nor cannot appoint or send any man to preach the gospel, yet we are glad that the Good Spirit has put it into the hearts of these Friends, to visit you in brotherly love.

"And we do approve and concur with our Friend John Parrish, in his present engagement to accompany our Friend Zebulon Heston, with sincere desires that the Good Spirit may be with them, and you, and prosper their way.

"We subscribe ourselves Your Friends.

"Signed in and on behalf of the Monthly Meeting of the people called Quakers, for the Northern District of Philadelphia, held at their meeting-house at the Bank, by adjournment, the 24th day of the Sixth Month, 1773.

"THOMAS MASTERMAN,	HEZEKIAH WILLIAMS,
THOMAS GILBERT,	SAML. NOBLE,
ROBERT PARRISH,	CHARLES WEST,
JOSEPH DRINKER,	DAVID ESTAUGH,
JOSEPH RAKESTRAW,	WILLIAM COWPER,
SAMUEL HOPKINS,	HENRY DRINKER,
JOSHUA EMLEN,	JOHN HUNT."
SAML. SANSOM,	

LETTER FROM REPRESENTATIVE COMMITTEE.

"*To Netawattwalemun and the rest of the Head men of the Delaware Indians at Kekaillammapaikung, and to John Papunehang, and the rest of the Indian brethren at Welhick, Thuppeek, and to all other Indians living beyond the Ohio, to whom these may come:*

"BRETHREN:—Your friends, the people called Quakers, in Pennsylvania and New Jersey often remember you with desires for your welfare and true happiness, and that the old friendship which was made between your fathers and ours, may still be maintained, and may ever continue between your and our children and grandchildren, from one generation to another; then it will always be pleasing to us to hear from, and to see one another.

"BRETHREN:—The several messages we received from you, by our brother Kilbuck, and Joseph Peepy, last year, and the year before, made deep impression on the minds of such of us, as were present when they were delivered, and have often since excited our thoughts of them. We, in our answers, informed you we were in hopes the love of God thro' our Lord and Saviour Jesus Christ, would engage and constrain some of the ministers of the gospel, to visit you, and until such should be thus sent among you, we desired you to attend diligently to the instructions of the Spirit of Christ within you, by which you may come to know your duty to God and one unto another.

"BRETHREN:—We are all of us unable rightly to obtain this saving knowledge, by our own wisdom and strength; we should therefore humbly, and diligently, wait for the Spirit of Christ to enlighten our minds, and to give us the right understanding, by which we may see that in a state of nature, we are weak, blind, and miserable, and can never come to a state of true happiness, without a Saviour; and if we receive this understanding, with thankful hearts, and sincerely desire the help of Christ, our Saviour, he will by the renewed working of His Good Spirit, instruct us more and more.

"BRETHREN:—The ministers of Christ, who are really led by his Spirit, and faithfully attend to His instructions, may be useful and a great help to others, by informing them what they have tasted and felt of His love, and when they speak from the constraints of that love, are often instrumental to raise the feeling sense of it in those to whom they speak, but all they can do, or should desire to do, is to bring men to Christ, that they may know and feel Him for themselves, as he is graciously manifesting Himself by His Spirit within them; for that which is to be known of God, is manifested within; and without this knowledge, no outward performance of any kind will work out their salvation, and bring them from a state of nature to a state of grace, wherein they may witness salvation, thro' the blood of Christ, which was shed for the redemption of all men.

"We fervently desire, you may come truly to know and experience this, every one of you, in and for yourselves, for no man can do this work for his brother, nor for his nearest friend.

"BRETHREN:—We write this to you, by our beloved Friend Zebulon Heston, whose mind being influenced with the love of Christ, and constrained thereby, engages him to go and visit you, being desirous, tho' an old man, to see you before he dies, and to express something of the goodness of God, which he hath known to preserve him from his youth to this day. He hath approved himself a faithful minister of Christ, both in word and doctrine, and in life and conversation, and we hope you will receive him, as our true friend and brother. As the journey is long, he is accompanied by our friend and brother, John Parrish, whose love to you is so great, that he is willing likewise, to go and see you. We sincerely desire and pray, that they may be ·instrumental to do you good, and that the blessing of God may attend you and them, and that you may shew forth to them, that first mark of the disciples of Christ, which is true love one unto another.

"Your desire of having some religious instructors for your children, we very heartily approve, and, as you have been before informed, whenever we can find any rightly qualified, and willing to undertake the service, we intend to assist and encourage them in it.

"The letter from Jno. Papunehang, and his brethren at Welhick, Thuppeek, was lately sent to some of us, by Jno. Etwein, and it is very pleasing to us, to hear of your prosperity and settlement there, the increase of which we sincerely desire.

"In much brotherly love we salute you and are your friends and brethren.

"Signed at a meeting of Friends, appointed to represent our Friends in Pennsylvania and New Jersey, held at Philadelphia, the 8th day of the Seventh Month, 1773.

"ISRL. PEMBERTON,	ANTHONY WILLIAMS,
WILLM. BROWN,	THOMAS HALLOWELL,
ANTHONY BENEZET,	DAVID ESTAUGH,
ISAAC ANDREWS,	JOSHUA MORRIS,
JOHN REYNELL,	JOHN ELLIOTT, JR.,
JAMS. PEMBERTON,	JOHN JONES,
JOHN PEMBERTON,	ISAAC PARRISH,
ABEL JAMES,	BENJAMIN HOOTON,
OWEN JONES,	CHARLES WEST,
SAML. EMLEN, JR.,	JOSEPH DRINKER,
JEREMIAH WARDER,	ROBERT PARRISH,
DAVID BACON,	ISAAC GRAY."

PHILADELPHIA YEARLY MEETING.

In 1761, the following minute appears :—" It being observed by the last epistle from the Meeting for Sufferings in London, that they express their approbation of the proceedings of those Friends here, who have been concerned in using their endeavors for the establishment of peace with the Indians by pacific measures, and warmly recommend, that a Christian regard and notice may be extended towards these people, for cultivating a good understanding with them, and the confirmation of peace,'on the principles of justice and equity:—Several suitable observations were now made thereupon, to excite Friends, individually, to a religious concern and care in this matter, more especially, as of late some good effects of a remarkable visitation of Divine Grace, has appeared among some of those people."

In 1763:—"On due consideration of the request from the Western Quarter, it is the solid sense and judgment of this meeting, that Friends should not purchase nor remove to settle such lands as have not been fairly and openly first purchased from the Indians, by those persons who are, or may be fully authorized by the Government, to make such purchases; and that Monthly Meetings, should be careful to excite their members to the strict observance of this advice; and where any remove, so contrary to the advice of their brethren, that they should not give certificates to such persons, but use their endeavors, to persuade them to avoid the danger to which they expose themselves, and to convince them of the inconsistency of their conduct, with our Christian profession."

In the extracts from the Minutes of the "Yearly Meeting for Pennsylvania, New Jersey, Delaware, and the eastern parts of Maryland and Virginia," held in Philadelphia from the 28th of Ninth Month to the 3d of Tenth Month, inclusive, 1795, is found, under date of Tenth Month 2d, the following:—

"The interesting concern, under which this meeting from time to time in years past, has been exercised, and wherewith the minds of many brethren have been so deeply affected, in relation to the former and present condition of the Indian natives, and with reference to events and occurrences respecting them, through a long course of years, being in a solid manner, at a preceding sitting, weightily revived, and spread with life over the meeting, to give the subject more fully that weight and deliberate consideration its importance calls for, a number of Friends were named; and also to report their sense, whether a fund might not be fitly appropriated, for the desirable purpose of promoting the civilization and well-being of the Indians, who now accordingly produced their report, which being read, is united with, being as follows, viz.:—

"'To the Yearly Meeting now sitting:—The Committee appointed on the interesting concern, for promoting the welfare of the Indian natives, report, that at several meetings, in which we have had the company of divers concerned brethren, not particularly named, to the service, we have deliberately considered this important subject, which hath for a series of years, deeply exercised the minds of many Friends, and been latterly, revived in the Yearly Meeting with increasing weight, our minds have been measurably drawn into sympathy with these distressed inhabitants of the wilderness; and on comparing their situation with our own, and calling to grateful remembrance the kindness of their predecessors to ours, in the early settlement of this country, considering also, our professed principles of peace and good-will to men, we were induced with much unanimity to believe, that there are loud calls for our benevolence and charitable exertions, to promote amongst them the principles of the Christian Religion, as well, as to turn their attention to school learning, agriculture, and useful mechanical employment; especially, as there appears in some of the tribes, a willingness to unite in the exercise of endeavors of this kind. We believe that this end may be much promoted under the Divine blessing, by a recommendation from this meeting, to the several Quarterly Meetings, that a liberal subscription be set on foot, and a fund raised, to be under the direction of a special committee, to be appointed by the Yearly Meeting, in order that these pious purposes may be carried into effect as early as practicable, and the apparent friendly disposition of Government, towards this desirable object improved. And conceiving that the subject is of sufficient magnitude, to claim the attention of our Religious Society, in different parts of this Continent, we think it may be useful, to hint the substance of this concern, in the Epistles to the respective Yearly Meetings.

"'Philadelphia, 2d of Tenth Month, 1795.

"'Signed, on behalf of the Committee, by several Friends.' "

Conformably whereto, a committee was appointed for the affecting of this beneficial purpose, viz. :—John Parrish, John Elliott, John Spencer, Jr., Anthony Johnson, John Stapler, Oliver Paxson, Joseph Trimble, James Emlen, Isaac Coates, Amos Hervey, Warner Mifflin, Samuel Howell, John Smith, Benjamin Clark, Benjamin Swett, John Hunt (of Evesham), James Cooper, Mark Miller, William Hartshorne, Richard Hartshorne, Thomas Wistar, Joseph Sansom, William Savery, John Biddle, Thomas Harrison, Henry Drinker, Joseph Sloan, John Pierce, John Hunt (of Darby).

FRIENDS' HISTORICAL ASSOCIATION

Has been organized for the purpose of collecting, and preserving from destruction and loss, the many books, papers, documents, and manuscripts of various kinds, which are known to be scattered about in different parts of the country.

Papers or documents of any kind, written or printed, bearing directly or indirectly upon the history of the Society of Friends, are solicited and will be thankfully received as donations; or any such material in the possession either of meetings or individuals, can be left with the Association for safe keeping; subject to the order of the persons so depositing them, so they can be reclaimed at any time.

The attention of all persons connected with or descended from members of the Society of Friends, is earnestly directed to this subject. The co-operation of all such is solicited, as it is believed that many papers of great value and interest can be thus secured and preserved from oblivion.

Address

FRIENDS' HISTORICAL ASSOCIATION,

820 Spruce Street, Philadelphia.